Just As I Am

PERSONAL PRAYERS FOR EVERY DAY

Ruth Etchells is a distinguished lay theologian who has combined the study of English literature and theology for much of her life. After teaching at a school in Liverpool and then training teachers at Chester College, she moved to university work in Durham in 1968. She founded the university course there in theology and literature and in 1978 was appointed Principal of St John's College with Cranmer Hall, thus becoming the first lay person and the first woman to be the head of a Church of England theological college.

She retired from university work in 1988 but still serves on the General Synod and Crown Appointments Commission. Her books include *Unafraid to Be* (1968) and, as editor, *Praying With the English Poets* (1990). The Archbishop of Canterbury conferred on her the Lambeth DD in 1992 for 'services to education, theological scholarship, and the work of the General Synod'.

Just As I Am

PERSONAL PRAYERS
FOR EVERY DAY

Ruth Etchells

TRIANGLE

First published in Great Britain 1994
Triangle Books
Society for Promoting Christian Knowledge
Holy Trinity Church
Marylebone Road
London NW1 4DU

British Library Cataloguing-in-Publication Data
A catalogue record for this book is available from the British Library

ISBN 0-281-04790-1

Typeset by Dorwyn Ltd, Rowlands Castle, Hants
Printed in Great Britain by BPC Paperbacks Ltd
Member of The British Printing Company Ltd

For the community

past, present, and future,

at

St John's College with Cranmer Hall

Durham,

thankfully

Contents

SEASONS AND FESTIVALS

TIMES OF SORROW, TIMES OF JOY

Foreword

Ruth's book *Unafraid to Be*, subtitled 'A Christian Study of Contemporary English Writing', exercised a profound effect on my thinking when I read it first twenty-five years ago. It opened up new vistas both of creative thought and of understanding as it reflected on the questions poets, playwrights, and novelists were wrestling with at the time.

At that stage I knew her only through her writing, but my years in Durham, coinciding as they did with some of the time she spent there, first as a lecturer and then as Principal of St John's College with Cranmer Hall, gave me the privilege of coming to know her as a personal friend.

Since then, both as Bishop of Bath and Wells, and in my present role, I have come to appreciate her wisdom more and more. Whether at General Synod, on the Doctrine Commission, or as a member of the Crown Appointments Commission, her contributions are always marked by clearly expressed thought combined with a great depth of pastoral and spiritual sensitivity.

This book enables us to view the powerhouse that lies within the person. It brings together her personal prayers and some of the resources she uses for her praying. But it does more than that. She has also aimed to provide a resource to help others in their prayers. My prayer is that will be the case, and that this collection of prayers will become the 'Personal Prayers' of many.

+ *George Cantuar*

Introduction

Whence it came

Daily personal prayer, disciplined and regular, is not something that most of us find easy. I find that my thoughts flitter about, that I embrace distraction, that sometimes it is with the utmost difficulty that I can make myself even begin; and the temptation to find either the place or the time inconvenient does not go away simply because that battle has been won on previous days.

Yet this personal dialogue with God is the very oxygen of our spiritual blood-stream, and without it we grow faint on the pilgrimage. It is a habit complementary to our regular coming together with fellow believers in public worship. There we rejoice in the richness of belonging together in Christ, rest on the extraordinary strength and potency of corporate prayer, and are caught up in the wonder of making together that offering of thanksgiving and praise, which is the common language of the people of God.

But though such public worship is a foretaste of things to come, our individual personal daily lives have to be lived out often far away from such mutualities. Yet it is vital for our soul's health that we know God here in our dailiness. And it is my own experience that without the practice of taking some time to talk with God in private, daily and personally, the intention of seeing the day through the lens of personal faith, and living it accordingly, is very hard to maintain with any consistency. It is like, as Ann Lewin put it, watching for the kingfisher:

> Prayer is like watching for the
> Kingfisher. All you can do is
> Be where he is likely to appear, and
> Wait.

Often, nothing much happens;
There is space, silence and
Expectancy.
No visible sign, only the
Knowledge that he's been there
And may come again.
Seeing or not seeing cease to matter,
You have been prepared.
But when you've almost stopped
Expecting it, a flash of brightness
Gives encouragement.*

This book of daily personal prayers, for morning and evening, is meant to help us 'be where he is likely to appear', which is indeed all we can do. God is most likely to appear in any ordinary moment of this day or night; and taking time to talk quietly to him, opening up our lives to him in the privacy of our own quiet place, means that — to quote the poem — we 'have been prepared'. For Christ is there where we do our living, our thinking, dreaming, hoping, loving, grieving, sinning, longing and giving; our worrying about all sorts of mundane matters, and our glimpsing of eternal things. So all these things need to be gathered up and offered daily, so that we can catch, from time to time, the flash of brightness which is his presence in them.

It is perfectly possible to do this, of course, without any bookish aid. But now we are back to that flitter-wittedness I lamented earlier. To combat that, my own daily prayer life was rooted and nourished for many years not only by daily Bible reading, which remains an essential, but also, to help focus personal praying, by John Baillie's *A Diary of Private Prayer*. That classic of personal prayer has nurtured many

*Ann Lewin, 'Disclosure', in *New Christian Poetry*, ed. Alwyn Marriage (Collins 1990).

thousands since it was first published in 1936, and it remains a wonderful resource, though indeed, as all prayer books do, it has become to some extent dated.

This book of personal prayers owes its inspiration to John Baillie and much of its structure. Its material, though, and its words, are mostly my own, the fruit of many years' daily conversation with God, often wrestling, sometimes resting, occasionally glorying, almost always — eventually — thanking. As such, the book is itself a thank-offering, to John Baillie to whom so many of us owe so much, and to the Lord he consistently drew us to.

How it may be used

This is emphatically not a book for public worship. It is for private — very private — prayer. Its basic structure is of thirty-one days of morning and evening prayers, together with a morning and an evening prayer for Sunday. There are also twelve prayers marking the Church's seasons and festivals, and nine 'theme' prayers for use in times of sorrow and of joy. These theme prayers are accompanied by page references indicating where amongst the daily cycle there are prayers which also touch on these themes. The intention here is that these theme prayers should fill out and balance the day's personal prayers where this would be appropriate; they are not intended to take the place of the daily prayer, which is why they are few in number.

For it is in the steady, cumulative effect of privately praying these very personal prayers, day after day, as a springboard to one's *own* voicing of one's *own* intimate praying, that I hope the book will be most helpful. For that reason I have included where possible a feature of Baillie's own prayer diary, a space at the end of each prayer where users can make prayer notes of their own. It may simply be a note of someone or some cause they want to pray for on that day every month. (Similarly the dashes in some prayers allow for mention of particular people and issues.) In my own case, I found that from time to time I noted down a particular moment that the day's prayers had marked in my life with God, of crisis or of great thanksgiving or of personal wrestling. Over the years, this personal record of past key moments of prayer got drawn into that day's monthly pattern of praying, enriching it with a vivid sense of personal pilgrimage.

It will not, however, always feel right to use the book for both morning and evening prayers. Sometimes just the mornings seem appropriate, sometimes it is the evening prayers that help most. The structure of the prayers does not assume that both are used in the day, but both are available.

These eighty-five daily prayers are, with some ten exceptions,* my own, newly composed, though long in the heart. To give them a memorable focus, I have used a short poem or prayer in most of them, drawn from fellow Christians ranging from the third century to today. (These are all listed in the Index of Authors at the back.) Often such quotations have been the springboard of my own prayers or their climax, and my hope is that they might be so for the users of this book also. They also serve to remind us continually of the marvellous richness of Christians' prayer through the ages, so that even when we pray alone, we touch fingers with the Church through time and space; and this is a marvellous antidote to becoming too introverted!

For personal praying is not at all, in the end, about oneself; it is about God, and about being thankfully or despairingly or joyfully or grievingly open to him. That is the only right end for a book like this: to help free us into the language of Christ, which is our proper tongue and our guide to our native city:

*See pages 42, 48, 52, 62, 84, 102, 120, 124, 150, 170.

Christ is a language in which we speak to God,
And also God, so that we speak in truth;
He in us, we in him, speaking
To one another, to him, the city of God.**

Ruth Etchells
Durham, 1994

**C.H. Sisson, in *Collected Poems*, (Carcanet 1984).

Lord . . .

My soul is so dry that by itself it cannot pray;
Yet you can squeeze from it the juice of a thousand prayers.
My soul is so parched that by itself it cannot love;
Yet you can draw from it boundless love for you and for my
neighbour.
My soul is so cold that by itself it has no joy;
Yet you can light the fire of heavenly joy within me.
My soul is so feeble that by itself it has no faith;
yet by your power my faith grows to a great height.
Thank you for prayer, for love, for joy, for faith;
Let me be always prayerful, loving, joyful and faithful.

Guigo the Carthusian[1]

Days

First Day · MORNING

Prayers for a First Day

O Lord God of every beginning and end, I bring this beginning to you now. Today I start another journey, a pilgrimage through an allotted space of time towards your great end of Love. Keep me safe through this pilgrimage, Lord; and so illuminate my spirit that I look always through the immediate, to see you at work in it, for your good purposes on the way and at my journey's end. So let me make this prayer of Boethius my own:

> O Father, give the spirit power to climb
> To the Fountain of all light and be purified.
> Break through the mists of earth, the weight of the clod,
> Shine forth in splendour, Thou that art calm weather
> And quiet resting place for faithful souls.
> To see Thee is the end and the beginning,
> Thou carriest us and Thou dost go before.
> Thou art the journey and the journey's end.
>
> *Boethius*[2]

And so, Lord, I make a commitment:

> I hand over to your care, Lord,
> my soul and my body
> my mind and thoughts
> my prayers and my hopes
> my health and my work
> my life and my death
> my parents and my family
> my friends and my neighbours
> my country and all people
> today and for ever. Amen.
> *Lancelot Andrewes*[3]

PRAYER NOTES

2/03/17 - Returning to work, apprehensive - asking God to help me see him at work in the immediate, & to break through the mists which cloud my vision, & the cloud = fear.

First Day · EVENING

O my God, I have no idea where I am going. Nor do I
really know myself, and the fact that I think I am
following your will does not mean that I am actually
doing so. But I desire to do your will, and I know the very
desire pleases you. Therefore I will trust you always
though I may seem to be lost. I will not fear, for you are
always with me, O my dear God.

Thomas Merton[4]

Lord, thank you that today the calender marked a fresh start.
May it have done so in my life. Let me put behind me all that
clogs my purpose of living for you; help me instead to take
strength from the certainty of your presence through this next
stretch of time.

As I look towards the possibilities and hopes that lie before
me, Lord, I think of those for whom this 'beginning again' has
brought no hope, only a sense of renewed anxiety or grief or
weariness or frustration. Especially I remember before you
tonight, Father, those nursing loved ones through long and
irreversible illnesses, those serving long prison sentences,
those caught in the grip of circumstances which seem wholly
intractable, those who are bereaved and grieving for a loss
which can never be assuaged, those who long for employment
and cannot find it. Father, into their darkness shed your mysterious light; ease and comfort and strengthen them, Lord
God of Gethsemane and the Cross.

And for those of us who fear that no new beginning can be
of use, give us your assurance that our very longing to begin
again is an offering you lovingly take to yourself, a worthy
prayer which delights you and on which you will build, if we
will let you. Lay now that foundation of assurance in my
heart and life, Father. Amen.

PRAYER NOTES

Second Day · MORNING

O Lord God, help me today to recognize how significant my life is, even when it seems obscure and unnoticed. Keep me conscious that I live it out in your presence, and that all I am and do matters infinitely, not just to me, but to you, and to the sum of good in your world.

So, dear Father, take my living today into your keeping. Give substance to my longing to serve you, deepen my understanding of you and your dealings with this world, and strengthen my will. Help me to a more deeply assured control of my thoughts and feelings, and the speech and action that flow from them: teach me to bring them constantly under your care. And Lord, stir me to a greater sensitivity to others. Show me the right way to serve them and you today; and so enlarge my heart that I may become less concerned for myself and my own needs and rights, and more concerned for those with whom I share the world.

Amongst these I pray especially for those who are of obvious significance in the world. I pray for those who have the responsibility of local government, here where I live; especially the Chief Executive and my own Council representative. I pray for the leaders of the church in this place, especially for those charged with the responsibility of guiding my own church. And I pray for those to whom I am answerable in my own tasks; where they bear heavy and hard responsibility may they be given wisdom, energy, patience, and humour; and loyal support by me.

Lord God, much of what comes to me today will not be what I would choose for myself. Yet all of it, prosaic and dull, glorious and exciting, or heart-breaking and soul-destroying, will be the arena of your love. Help me to recognize it as such, and so make this day a day of obedience, of spiritual peace, even of joy; make the way I live today a little part of the work of the kingdom of our Lord Jesus Christ, in whose name I pray. Amen.

⁓

PRAYER NOTES

Second Day · EVENING

Christ beneath me, Christ above me,
Christ in quiet, Christ in danger,
Christ in hearts of all that love me,
Christ in mouth of friend or stranger.
St Patrick[5]

Lord Christ, as I look back over today I am conscious that where I got things wrong I had taken my eyes off you: like Peter floundering in the seas when he tried to do the impossible without your strong hand. And where things seemed to go right, Lord, I was conscious of you at work.

So now at the end of the day I place in your keeping all I have met and done today:

— all the people I have met: in casual encounters; in long talks; at home; in doing things together; in dispute; in affection; in distress; in shared hopes.

Especially I remember ____ and ____ and ____.

Forgive, Lord, anything amiss I have said or done today, alone or towards others, and help me where possible to set it right. I think especially of ____ and ____. And thank you, too, for ____ and ____; and keep me more and more aware of other people's goodness.

And I offer to you:

— all today's plans or decisions or actions;
all today's thinking or dreaming or hoping or fearing.

Help me to hold all these under your will, Lord Christ, so that I do not go rushing heedlessly and self-deceivingly down the road of self-will.

Especially I remember my dreams and plans about ____ and ____.

Dear Lord, I thank you that everything in this universe is under your hand; and that you are behind and before me, above and below me, there in the silence and there in the noise, there in my loneliness and there when I am companied. Everywhere and always, you are there. Thank you, Lord. Amen.

PRAYER NOTES

Third Day · MORNING

Christ is the morning star
who when the darkness of this world is past
   brings to his saints
the promise of the light of life
   and opens everlasting day.

The Venerable Bede[6]

Lord God of light, I praise you for the gift of darkness, for the night that has just passed; for ordaining the rhythm of sleep and waking in your creatures. And I thank you, Lord, that you have kept me safely through these hours of darkness, given me sleep and been with me when the hours have seemed long.

And I praise you, Lord God of the dark, for the gift of light, for this new day with its possibilities as well as its duties. Thank you that each dawn is a symbol of renewal, a fresh chance, a reminder that your universe will always be starred with your light and its hope.

Lord God, thank you for the gift of Christ who like the morning star in the long dark night gives certain promise that the dawn will come, our weariness and fears be assuaged, in this life and in eternity. Help me to hold on to this certainty as an act of faith when the darkness of my life seems endless and full of threat. Help me to hold on to it even through the darkness of death itself.

And, Lord, I pray for those to whom this morning light brings no sense of renewal, but instead more weariness, more pain, more anxiety, more loss. O loving Lord of light and darkness, renew hope within them, and let them glimpse your morning star. For Christ's sake. Amen.

PRAYER NOTES

Third Day · EVENING

Now, my heavenly Father, as my day ends I turn thankfully to you. Recall to me that each day begins, continues and ends in you. This morning it was in your grace I set out: forgive me if I faced too carelessly without you what the day would bring. All day I have experienced activity and stillness, encounters and absences, which are alike the arena of your love. So I look back over the day and give you thanks, and ask forgiveness, and pray for prospering.

> *Thank you*, Father, for various tasks done or begun, for relationships furthered or set right, for sights or sounds or incidents which gave joy.
> Particularly I thank you for ＿＿ and ＿＿ and ＿＿.

> *Forgive me*, Father, for thoughts or words or acts which were unwise, unnecessary, untruthful, unkind, or ungenerous.
> Particularly forgive me for ＿＿ and ＿＿ and ＿＿.

> *Prosper*, Father, all that was done right today, and all those whose lives I have shared in today.
> Particularly I ask your blessing on ＿＿ and ＿＿ and ＿＿.

And tonight I remember before you:

— all who are overworked; all who cannot get work; and all whose work is not appreciated;
— all who today have heard hard news, faced great loss, or suffered sharp anxiety or been oppressed by dreadful fear;
— all who suffer great pain, or who are tonight facing a major operation; or who know their illness is terminal; or who bear the aching weariness of old age.

12

O Lord Christ, who worked and was weary; whose efforts were rejected; and who bore great suffering, even to the death agony; comfort the comfortless through your great mercy. Amen.

PRAYER NOTES

Fourth Day · MORNING

Protect, O Lord, from thoughts without action
Guard, O Lord from words without feelings
Defend, O Lord, from ideas without results
And surround me with your Presence.

David Adam[7]

O Living God, in whose presence I begin my own day's living, I thank you that you are in charge of today, and that I am utterly known and understood by you. You guide and lead me in the way that I should go, because you love me and my whole world.

So, my Father, I bring to you my life today. I long to make it an offering to you, as a day well lived. But I so often use my time wastefully or self-indulgently. So today, Father, help me:

— to turn vague good intentions into concrete action;
— to follow up ideas with the toil that makes them work;
— to keep my tongue from time-wasting,
   from self-indulgent gossip,
   from careless and insensitive words,
   from self-display.

O loving Father, how little I can achieve myself! But let me draw hope and strength minute by minute from your presence surrounding me and your love overshadowing me. And so, putting behind me all sense of inadequacy, let me glory today in the wonder of your love for us, the wisdom of your work for us, and the power of your purposes for us. In the name of our Lord Jesus whom you gave for us, let me share this day with others as a day you have made for us, in which to rejoice in your life and love. And so keep us thankful. Amen.

PRAYER NOTES

Fourth Day · EVENING

Lord of all, now as my day closes I give you thanks for everything in it.

A United Nations General Secretary once wrote:

> 'Night is drawing nigh':
>> For everything that has been, thanks,
>> To everything that will be, yes.
>>> *Dag Hammarskjöld*[8]

Help me to pray that prayer tonight, Lord.

I thank you
— for every human contact today, slight or profound, happy or disturbing; and I remember before you tonight especially ____ and ____ and what we have done and said together. Forgive anything dishonouring to you or each other, and bless and foster everything good.

I thank you
— for all the smaller things that gave today its character: the weather, the morning mail, the family's doings, our food and drink, the world beyond my window, the radio and TV I have enjoyed or been challenged by. Help me to savour all that has been good, and to handle in your name all that was ill.

Be with those in great need tonight, Lord Christ, those who face agony of body or spirit, loss, bereavement, loneliness or terror. Be a stilling presence in their storm. May this prayer be an offering for those who cannot themselves pray. And when, O Lord, to me too, such things come, may I have so steadily prayed this prayer of thankfulness and trust in times of quiet, that your presence is sure to me when my own soul's night is drawing nigh. Help me to say then, even as I do now as I lie down in peace to sleep, 'In the name of Jesus

Christ, for everything that has been, thanks; to everything that will be, yes.'

PRAYER NOTES

Fifth Day · MORNING

The Father has put us into the world,
not to walk through it with lowered eyes,
but to search for him through things,
  events, people.
Everything must reveal God to us.

Michel Quoist[9]

O marvellous Lord, I cannot see you with my eyes or touch you with my hands, as your first followers tell us they did; yet today grant me such a strong conviction of your reality and power that I recognize you in all things. When I go out from here to the dailiness of my life, keep alive in me the sense that you are everywhere to be seen if I will only look with my heart. I shall live my life today in space and time: yet help me to hold fast to the truth that I also live it in your eternity. Make me brave enough to face any changes in my way of life and scale of values that such a vision may require. So help me today to seek not so much for success or achievement or acquisitions or power or status, as for the fruits of your Spirit in your world and in my own life: love, joy, peace, gentleness, truthfulness . . .

And I thank you, Father, for all the ways you have shown yourself to others in the past, who have loved and obeyed you: not just the great saints and prophets, but ordinary men and women like myself. You have always been there in the beauty and mystery of our natural world, and you are there too in all that is good in our daily life, especially in family attachments and wherever love is shown. You are there in all human encounters, in vast gatherings and in private converse. And you were supremely there in that moment of our human history when our Lord Jesus accepted death for our sake, and defeated it. So let me delight in your presence in everything

today, Lord God, and draw strength from it. In the name of
Jesus Christ. Amen.

PRAYER NOTES

Fifth Day · EVENING

Blind unbelief is sure to err
And scan his works in vain
God is his own interpreter
and he will make it plain.
William Cowper[10]

Lord, I have struggled so long, and I cannot find sense in it: so much terrible suffering in your world, so much wicked cruelty unchecked, so many innocent lives blighted or maimed by disaster, disease, war, famine, violence, greed, sectarian or ethnic hatred, or by sheer casual selfishness. Lord, the bad prosper: and innocent ones suffer.

Lord, I cannot bear it, and I cannot bear that you allow it.

And then I look at you again, Lord. And I see
— not the all-powerful King in glory
— not the mighty Creator of the Universe,

but you, Lord,

— misunderstood by your closest friends
— betrayed by one you had a right to trust
— seized and manacled and hustled
— spat on and struck and flogged
— publicly stripped and humiliated
— strung up tight on an agonizing cross
— dying of thirst, heat, suffocation, shock, exhaustion and agony . . .

Lord, the bad prospered, and the innocent one suffered.

And you took it into yourself, and showed us indestructible life, indestructible love, more powerful and more glorious than any prosperity among the bad. Help me, Lord, always to prefer your way to your enemies' way, your cross to their triumph. And challenge me, sharply, to *trust* God, as you did;

20

to trust that God will interpret all things for me, and make them plain.

So give me faith and love till I have sight, Lord. Amen.

———

PRAYER NOTES

Sixth Day · MORNING

> Before what cradle
> do those travellers from afar,
> strontium and plutonium, hold out
> their thin gifts?
> What anthems have our computers
> to insert into the vacuum caused
> by the break in transmission
> of the song upon Patmos?
> *R. S. Thomas*[11]

Father God, when I look at the world I live in I am sometimes very frightened by the technological powers we are wielding while we are so unable to rule our souls. So this morning, Father, I pray for my world:

— for all scientists, that they may combine zeal in research with real care for its implications for the world and its peoples;

— for world politicians, that they may be delivered from self-seeking and the short view; and that they may recognize they hold the world in trust;

— for all of us who feel helpless and powerless as we see the dangers to our world which we seem unable to influence.

Creator Lord, I thank you for the mystery and marvel of your universe, and for my place in it. I thank you for those in the past who have worked with its physical and spiritual laws to create beauty, fruitfulness and order. I pray for my generation, that we might hand on to our successors a world better for our having lived in it. Help me not to discount my own small part in that, Lord. And to maintain my share of the song on Patmos. Amen.

PRAYER NOTES

Sixth Day · EVENING

Be off, Satan, from this door and from these four walls.
There is no place for you, there is nothing for you to do
here. This is the place for Peter and Paul and the holy
gospel; and this is where I mean to sleep, now that my
worship is done, in the name of the Father and the Son
and the Holy Spirit.
One of the earliest Christian prayers recorded[12]

Father God, I thank you that through the centuries we have
been able to bring to you our worst fears, and claim the
certainty of your protection. Help me now, Father, as I end
the day, to turn out of this room all that is inimical to your
peace in my soul:

— against fear of bodily harm or night
  intruder, *I set the victory of Christ*;
— against fear of the supernatural, of
  mysterious and unexplained terrors,
  I set the victory of Christ;
— against the guilt of things ill done by me
  today or in the past, that burden my heart,
  I set the victory of Christ;
— against fear of my own weakness in the
  night's temptations, *I set the victory of
  Christ*;
— against fears for those I love, of threats
  to their safety and well-being, *I set the
  victory of Christ*;
— against fears for my country and the wider
  world, the darkness of human history and
  its possible end, *I set the victory of
  Christ*.

So may I lie down to sleep in peace, in the name of the Father, the Son and the Holy Spirit. Amen.

PRAYER NOTES

Seventh Day · MORNING

> Lord . . .
> May your bounty teach me
> greatness of heart.
> May your magnificence
> stop me being mean.
> Seeing you a prodigal
> and open-handed giver
> let me give unstintingly
> like a King's son
> like God's own.
> *Archbishop Helda Camara*[13]

O amazing God, what a world and what activity you call us to! Thank you for your gifts of energy and vision. Probing the stars, exploring the sea-bottom, digging back into our ancient past, computerising the future, harnessing the laws of nature, identifying the deepest patterns by which we live: social, economic, psychological, moral, political; and enlarging our understanding of them and of your spiritual law undergirding them all. Thank you, Lord God of the Universe, for the magnificence of that spiritual law by which we ultimately live.

Inspire in me increasingly that prodigality of spirit which is the mark of your grace, and the gift of our Lord Jesus Christ. Today, Father:

— in all my dealings save me from meanness:
  let me give unstintingly, like God's own;
— in all my tasks help me work committedly:
  let me give unstintingly, like God's own;
— in all my relationships teach me generosity
  let me give unstintingly, like God's own.

O Lord, behind the ordinariness of today let me recognize and grow up in the wonder and power of your law. And be especially with those today for whom disappointment, bereavement, weariness or sickness make even simple survival a struggle. Give them glimpses, Father, of your glory enfolding them. For Christ who gave all. Amen.

PRAYER NOTES

Seventh Day · EVENING

> God, of your goodness, give me yourself; for you are
>   enough for me.
> I cannot properly ask anything less, to be worthy of you,
> If I were to ask less, I should always be in want,
> In you alone do I have all.
>
>

Julian of Norwich[14]
>

O Father God, all day I have been signalling my needs to you. Crying out for help when the pressure got too great and I was near to breaking because of the demands on me: people, people, Lord, people clutching at my attention endlessly, their demands sucking up my energy. And time, time, Lord, never enough time to get everything done, and the misery of things not done properly. And now body and spirit are so achingly weary that I can hardly bother to prepare for bed. Lord, I ache so, and feel so diminished . . . Surely a life of true service is not meant to be like this? Is it? Crucifixion by a thousand little pins on a small plywood cross?

O my Lord, of your goodness, give me yourself in my weariness: let me walk in my mind with you through the day, and recognize where you were in each bit of it. And as I do, give me yourself in it, so that I can worship you there at that very moment.

I think of ____ among the people I was with; and ____ among what happened. God of goodness, give me yourself especially in the moments I found hard to bear.

As I lie down to rest now I ask you to give me yourself while I sleep, so that when I wake, I shall be still with you. Take my weariness, Lord, as an offering to you for those to whom I can give nothing else. But in you is all the gift that any of us need. Help me to trust that, and so rest in peace. Amen.

PRAYER NOTES

Eighth Day · MORNING

Let us praise our Maker, with true passion extol him.
Let the whole creation give out another sweetness,
Nicer in our nostrils, a novel fragrance
. . . .
Phenomena and numbers announcing in one
Multitudinous ecumenical song
Their grand givenness of gratitude and joy.

W. H. Auden[15]

O Lord God Almighty, I thank you for this world of beauty
and delight, and for your promise that it will be redeemed of
all that despoils and distresses it.
   I thank you:

— for all there is to see and hear and wonder at in your
   world;
— for the delight and beauty of the natural world, and the
   fascination and energy of the city;
— for creatures various and strange, or familiar and
   companionable;
— for the joy of trusted friendship, and the pleasure of
   new contacts;
— for the intimacies of love, of marriage, of families in
   their many diverse forms;
— for music and drama and films and radio and television
   in their excellence;
— for tasks to do, waged or unwaged, and the strength
   and will to do them;
— for a home to shelter in and to share;
— for the fellowship of your people and the joy of worship
   together.

Forgive me, Lord, that I have not always guarded the Earth's
resources, protected its creatures, appreciated the richness of

the civilization I lived in, or cared for those for whom these joys are barren. Keep me mindful that all that is good here is in trust, and that I have a debt to those who will follow. And by your grace keep me from so losing myself in the joys of earth that I lose sight of the greater joys of heaven. For which, dear Lord, prepare me. Amen.

PRAYER NOTES

Eighth Day · EVENING

Think through me, thoughts of God;
My Father, quiet me,
Till in Thy holy presence, hushed
I think Thy thoughts with Thee.
Amy Carmichael[16]

Now as the day ends, Father, let me put off all its swirling hopes and disappointments, its little victories and its small but bitter defeats, strip them away, as I strip off today's tired clothes:

— my Father, quiet me.

And in this quiet, Father, tune me in to your presence, so that the crackling and atmospherics of my own beating mind and soul die away, and in the clearness your thoughts crystallize in my soul.

Let me open my hands, and drop all the urgencies I was going to press on you: all the injuries I was wanting you to attend to, all the proud moments — poor, poor proud moments — I was going to display to you; even the needs of friends I was going to urge on you. Help me to open the hands of my heart and drop them, Lord, all of them:

— my Father, quiet me.

And in this quiet, Father, as your thoughts take shape in my soul, may they become so deeply a part of me that I start to think them with you: quietly, deeply, in harmony with you, help me to think the thoughts of God:

— my Father. Your name is Love.

PRAYER NOTES

Ninth Day · MORNING

There's only what you do.
Everything else is inside your head.

But what you do is just the expression
of who you are
and what you know.

And what you do covers a multitude of sins.
You do your tone of voice
. . . .
You do the silences between your words
as well as the words themselves.
You do the songs you sing.
You do the cup of tea you made your mum.
You do the way you spend your money
and the way you didn't spend it.
You do the love you make
and all the love you didn't make.
You do the atmosphere you change within a room.
You do the rocking of the baby in your arms
. . . .

But . . . what you do is the expression
of who you are
and what you know.

If what you are feels wrong or not worth much
scrunched up in a miserable little ball,
It goes without saying that what you do will mirror that.
And what others do you will receive
much the same.

Kathy Galloway[17]

O God of Love, my heart so often feels like a heavy cold stone
within me, and I cannot feel the warmth and truth of your

love for me, or know I am of any value, or respond with a joy and hope that melt all that hardness inside. Give me, now, the grace to open myself to you: this morning let me face those barriers within myself which shut out your love, and accept it fully in thankfulness:

— trusting you that its demand will not be
  too great for my frailty;
— letting its healing warmth teach me of my
  great worth in your eyes,

so that all I do and am is shaped by it. And let me see all that others do in the light of that love. So may the love I 'do' today shine with the love in which you have secured me. Amen.

~

PRAYER NOTES

Ninth Day · EVENING

The loveliest thing earth hath, a shadow hath
A dark and livelong hint of death,
Haunting it ever till its last faint breath

. . . .

Who then may tell
The beauty of heaven's shadowless asphodel?
Walter de la Mare[18]

O my Father God, today has been such a good day, that I do not want it to end. Thank you for all its richness: for sunlight through my window, for its loveliness on all it touches — leaf and bough and flower and the curtains and furnishings of this home you have given me.

Thank you for family and friends. For laughter and doing things together and the opening of mind and heart to each other and to you. For tasks to do and the strength to do them. For kindnesses. For the challenge to read and hear and view and to think, clearly and truthfully and deeply. For the creatures we share the world with, particularly those in and near our homes, birds, fish, cats, dogs, goats, horses; and the gift of their beauty, innocence and trust. For encounters in the shopping centre, in the workplace, in the leisure centre, that have made the day richer. For goals achieved or worked towards. For the love of those dearest to me, and for their well-being.

O Father, it has been such a good day, I want to hold it for ever and not lose it. So all this richness is touched with loss, Father; and tonight I feel my mortality, the truth that everything passes, nothing lasts, we and the world are all transient.

And then I ponder on the mystery of your love, and know that it never fades or changes. Because of that, in Browning's words, 'There never shall be one lost good.' And so I lie down to sleep in safety, knowing today's joys are fingerposts to heaven. Thank you, Father. Amen.

PRAYER NOTES

Tenth Day · MORNING

They shall not hurt or destroy in all my holy mountain
Isaiah 11.9. NEB

No hurt, Lord? no destruction? anywhere? your word —
Word — on it? This morning as I look round my world, I so
passionately long for that life you have promised when
violence shall cease and we treat each other and the creatures around us with respect and tenderness. When we no
longer force others to our own way by aggression or
brutality or simply superior strength; no longer treat
those who share the world with us as stumbling blocks to
our own will, or resources for us to suck dry and then
discard.

O Lord God, though I groan in spirit that we do these
things, yet I confess I am part of them. I too have wanted my
own way and been aggressive or ruthless to achieve it. I too
have wanted a quality of comfort in life only possible at too
high a price for this planet's good.

So today, Father, help me to take with me into all my
thinking and living, doing and being, alone or with others,
this vision of your holy hill of peace which is promised us. Let
me look through each situation I am in to that peace you shed
on it from within; so that I respond in the light of that peace,
instead of from my own self-will.

And when I find that impossible, Lord God, then let me
cling for help to the Lord Jesus, who being in very nature
God, yet did not consider equality with God something to be
grasped, but made himself nothing, taking the very nature of a
servant, being made in human likeness. And being found in
appearance as a man, he humbled himself and became obedient to death — even death on a cross.

So let me tap into Christ's secret of peace whatever its cost to me; and so discover your holy mountain for myself and others. Amen.

~

PRAYER NOTES

Tenth Day · EVENING

He who has seen me has seen the Father
John 14.9 RSV

Lord God, through my window the night sky is so vast, and, to my ordinariness, incomprehensible. Beautiful, but mysterious, beyond awe almost to fear. And when I try to grasp with my mind what that reveals about you, Lord, Creator of the night skies and of worlds and dark spaces far beyond, then I am lost and afraid in the vastness of your mystery.

How can I dare even to address a Being responsible for all that? How can I attach much worth or significance to this tiny planet Earth, and to its creaturely life, in the scale of all that vastness?

Can it really be, Lord God, that I can know you, and that you want me to know you, and that you have provided a means for me to know you? Not know *about* you, O Holy God, but actually meet you, begin to trust you, learn to love you . . . ? How profound beyond my imagining must be the quality of the way you love your inconceivably vast creation, when you provide for such needs as me and mine.

But, 'that which was from the beginning . . . we have heard . . . we have seen with our eyes . . . we have touched . . .' So I turn in great thankfulness, to the One you have given us to help us know you, Holy God. I thank you for the Lord Jesus, who shows us his bleeding hands and says 'This is the Lord your Creator, the Holy God'; who shows us healing; who confronts hypocrisy, self-righteousness, cruelty, greed and selfishness; who is infinitely tender to those who suffer and grieve: the self-doubting, those miserable with guilt, the wounded, the burdened, the of-no-account: and says, 'This is the Lord your Creator, the Holy God'; who endured every horror, for the world he loved: and says, 'This is the Lord your Creator, the Holy God'; whose dynamic love was

40

stronger than death itself, so that he is with us now, active and redeeming in this night.

Lord of the vast night skies, let me dwell constantly on what you have shown me in Christ Jesus of yourself, the 'Love that moves the sun and the other stars'. Amen.

PRAYER NOTES

41

Eleventh Day · MORNING

On Waking

Living Lord, you have watched over me, and put your hand on my head, during the long dark hours of night. Your holy angels have protected me from all harm and pain. To you, Lord, I owe life itself. Continue to watch over me and bless me during the hours of day.

On Rising

Rule over me this day, O God, leading me on the path of righteousness. Put your Word in my mind and your Truth in my heart, that this day I neither think nor feel anything, except what is good and honest. Protect me from all lies and falsehood, helping me to discern deception whenever I meet it. Let my eyes always look straight ahead on the road you wish me to tread, that I might not be tempted by any distraction. And make my eyes pure, that no false desires be awakened within me.

On Going to the Day's Tasks

Give me, dear Lord, a pure heart and a wise mind, that I may carry out my tasks according to your will. Save me from all false desires, from pride, greed, envy and anger, and let me accept joyfully every task you set before me. Let me seek to serve the poor, the sad, and those unable to work. (And when I cannot work myself, Lord, keep me fruitful and free from bitterness.) Help me to discern honestly my own gifts that I may do the things of which I am capable, and happily and humbly leave the rest to others. Above all, remind me constantly that I have nothing except what you give me, and can do nothing except what you enable me to do. Amen.

Jacob Boehme (adapted)[19]

PRAYER NOTES

Eleventh Day · EVENING

If he is Judge to pass sentence on his servant,
He is also Lord to protect his servant,
Creator, to watch over his handiwork,
And God, to save those who believe in Him and are his
baptised.

Anselm of Canterbury[20]

O Glorious God, shining in the light of holiness, as this day ends I feel stained and soiled with weariness and failure. I know that today:

— my tongue was uncontrolled
— my patience wore thin
— I thought ungenerously of others
— I gave way to self-righteous anger
— I spoke loftily and behaved basely
— I used other people for my own ends
— I surrendered to my desires knowing them wrong
— I turned from your blessing.

O Lord my judge, I confess with shame. I am truly sorry, and I long for your forgiveness.

And I thank you, my loving Father, that you are my protector as well as my judge, taking from me this load of failure and burying it in Christ's tomb, where it can no longer harm me. And that you are our Creator God, hating nothing you have made but rejoicing in it all — even me. And that you give me the precious gift of sharing your delight in, and care for, your handiwork. Thank you, Lord, for its beauty, delicacy and glory; and for allowing me to share in your watch over Creation. And above all, Lord, you are our saving God, active within our history to bring us home to you. So let me rest tonight free from myself, thinking not of my failures or fears or even hopes, but of your great love in Christ, of the certainty of your protective care, and of those with whom I can share it, and of how I may share it. For Christ's sake. Amen.

PRAYER NOTES

Twelfth Day · MORNING

The best prayer is to rest in the goodness of God,
knowing that that goodness can reach right down to our
lowest depth of need.

Julian of Norwich[21]

God of the morning, as I wake to another day and prepare for
what may lie before me, I know only 'goodness' can keep this
world and my soul through the long hours; and not my goodness, Lord, nor any human goodness, except as it expresses
yours. So in this moment of preparation I bind to myself the
grace of *your* goodness, that it may sink into the very depths
of my being, and purge, heal and strengthen,

— transforming how I hear and see
— shaping what I do and am.

And Lord, I pray for my world, which in so many ways rejects
your goodness, or shrugs it away, or ignores it. O Father God,
forgive us, blind or stupid or self-centred or lazy or arrogant
as we are, that we do not recognize our need, and the things
which would make for our peace.

So today, Lord, I pray for:

— those who glimpse your goodness, but fear its demands
  on their lives, and so turn away.
  Especially I think of ____;
— those who have been so hardly used, so badly hurt in
  life, that they cannot trust in anything, cannot believe
  in 'good'.
  Especially I think of ____;
— those in positions of leadership and power, whose
  philosophies shape our nation: that they may test their
  policies by the rule of your goodness, and challenged by

it, may never persuade themselves that ill is good.
Especially I think of _____, Prime Minister, and all Cabinet members.

Finally, O Lord, I commit to your goodness all those I love, that their souls and hearts may be kept in that safest of all securities. Amen.

PRAYER NOTES

Twelfth Day · EVENING

Glory to Thee, my God this night
For all the blessings of the light;
Keep me, O keep me, King of Kings
Beneath thine own almighty wings.

Forgive me, Lord, for thy dear Son,
The ill that I this day have done,
That with the world, myself and thee
I ere I sleep at peace may be.

Teach me to live that I may dread
The grave as little as my bed;
Teach me to die, that so I may
Rise glorious at the aweful day.

O may my soul on thee repose,
And with sweet sleep my eyelids close,
Sleep that may me more vigorous make
To serve my God when I awake.

When in the night I sleepless lie,
My soul with heavenly thoughts supply;
Let no ill dreams disturb my rest,
No powers of darkness me molest.
                              Thomas Ken[22]

Let it be so, Lord, for your name's sake; trusting in which, I
will lay me down in peace and take my rest; for it is thou,
Lord, only, that makest me dwell in safety.

PRAYER NOTES

Thirteenth Day · MORNING

The prayer of the goat

Lord,
let me live as I will!
I need a little wild freedom,
a little giddiness of heart,
the strange taste of unknown flowers
. . . .
I love to bound to the heart of all
Your marvels,
leap Your chasms
and, my mouth stuffed with intoxicating grasses,
quiver with an adventurer's delight
On the summit of the world! Amen.

Carmen Bernos de Gasztold[23]

O marvellous Lord, give me a spirit of marvelling! Let me make my own this 'prayer of the goat', that instead of dully taking things for granted, routinely staying in safe well travelled ways, I may venture ever further into the marvel at the heart of your love. Inspire in me a spirit of delight and adventure in discovering new territories of grace. Let me be prepared to pay the price of effort, courage, and change in myself and my circumstances that such adventuring forward in the world of your love may bring.

And, Lord, sensitize me where I am resistant to others who do this: forgive me that I want to stay over-safely within known ways. I am so fearful of our straying like lost sheep, that I sometimes close my heart to the special gifts and vision you are inspiring in others. Remind me constantly of my Lord Jesus Christ's struggle to lead hearts into a richer and more marvellous adventure with you. So take away my defensiveness, Lord, that I may judge truly between irresponsibility and new vision, between anarchic self-satisfaction and divine prompting. And let me so delight in others' gifts and understanding that they may become for me a path to ever greater marvels of your grace. Amen.

———

PRAYER NOTES

Thirteenth Day · EVENING

O Lord God, the only source of all that is good and fair and true, I come thankfully at the end of the day to you.

— O God, here and now enter my heart.
   Now as I pray this prayer, do not let me furtively close any room within it.
— O God, enable me always to pursue the good.
   Now as I pray this prayer, let there be no secret purpose of wrong forming in me awaiting its opportunity.
— O God, bless and prosper my concerns and activities.
   Now as I pray this prayer, let there be nothing I am planning on which I dare not ask your blessing.
— O God, give me chastity of heart, mind and body.
   Now as I pray this prayer, let me not be saying secretly, 'But not yet because I am not ready'; or 'But no more than is reasonable in these times'.
— O God, bless everyone in this household and in my wider circle of friends.
   Now as I pray this prayer, let me not be still harbouring feelings of jealousy, anger or bitterness towards any of them. And if the truth is that I am, Lord, then help me to want passionately not to be, and so to offer it all now to your astringent love for purging and redeeming.
— O God, bless with your grace those who feel enmity to me, and those who have done me wrong.
   Now as I pray this prayer, let me not still cherish in my heart a hope that they will be requited.
— O God, establish your rule in all the earth.
   Now as I pray this prayer, let me not be still intending to devote my own best energies and hours to the service of my own interests.

O Spirit of the living God, as I now go to my rest, let that mind be in me which was also in Christ Jesus. Amen.

John Baillie (freely adapted)[24]

PRAYER NOTES

Fourteenth Day · MORNING

O God, my God
I praise you now for your hand on all my life:

> for my conception and safe birth;
> for my nurturing through childhood;
> for education and for leisure skills;
> for tenderness and love in my family and beyond.

> For my dreams of what my life might be;
> for this civilisation in which I live, and my civil rights within it;
> for such gifts of mind and person as I have, and some opportunities to use them.

> For the work I have been able to do, and your sustaining in its heaviness and toil;
> for your presence with me in unemployment, sustaining me in its emptiness and rejection.

> For the times when money has been short, and you have met my need;
> for the times when my income has been high, and you have taught me generosity and stewardship.

> For love in relationships, and for the wonder of mutual commitment;
> for the mysterious gift of marriage: the hopefulness of homemaking, the joys of physical intimacy, the slow learning of self-sacrifice and the glory of faithfulness.

> For children, the wonder and joy of them, and all the fears and hopes for them;
> for the renewing gift of their love, and your comfort when that disappoints.

> For the companionship of friends, its tenderness and depth;
> for comfort in desolate bereavement.

For the pleasure of health and energy, and the care of doctors and nurses when they fail.

For your beautiful world, with its creatures, and the challenge to conserve it and them.

For far cities and strange peoples and the richness in learning of them.

For all simple joys; all gentle thoughts; all music, books, films and art which feed the mind and nourish the soul.

For your church, in its many forms; for all who truly worship the one true God.

For the experience of the love of Christ in my life; for the joy of all who know him.

For the experience of eternal things in this life, and the hope of heaven hereafter.

O God, my God, how shall I thank you? with all my heart? Yes, Lord. Amen.

PRAYER NOTES

Fourteenth Day · EVENING

Father . . .
keep us so close to Your heart
that even our dreams are peaceful,
and that we may see things

. . . .

more and more from your point of view.
Corrie Ten Boom[25]

O loving and comforting Father, it has been such a hard day that I could not stay focused on you. Help me now to come so close to you that my foggy sight clears, and you are there, lucid and loving in my life. So let me try to understand the bad bit of the day in the light of your love.

Today, Father, I was badly wounded. People were not only rude but hurtful so that I felt battered and diminished and misjudged. The pain of staying silent, Lord . . . And my anger and pain went on darkening my day; and O, Lord, as I tell you about it I feel the tears from my sense of being wronged rising up within me.

Let me look again at it, Lord, with the eyes of your love:

— You ask me, Lord: why does it matter so much that others misjudge me? — I *hurt*, Lord!

— Is it perhaps *not* my passion for justice which makes me weep, but my tender sensitivity about my own standing? — Yes, Lord; true, Lord. But still I mind . . .

— You ask me, Lord: do I think that God thinks less of me because of what was said? — No, Lord; the reverse. But still I grieve . . .

— You ask me, Lord: do I know you love me? And that every struggle on my part to follow Christ's way in the face of unkindness or misunderstanding is a source of deep and loving joy to you? That heaven is the richer for my struggles today? That today I entered just a little more into the fellowship of generous and selfless love whose name is discipleship and whose heart is the Cross?

— The Cross. . . . I am ashamed of my grief. For yes, my Lord, I look at it and I *know* you love me; and as I look at you when I say that, I know nothing in life or death matters more than that. The wounds remain, but, salved by you, their sting is gone. O my Lord, stay like this, lucid and loving in my heart tonight. Amen.

PRAYER NOTES

Fifteenth Day · MORNING

Lord of the morning, I do not want to rise and face this day. I am so weary of the endless round of tasks, of its tedium, of the lack of encouragement or appreciation, the weariness of grinding routine, the draining impact of constant petty criticism. And I feel so confined, Lord, by the lack of space for myself and my dreams. I feel a prisoner in my own life. Somewhere there must be freedom and light and gaiety and delight and stimulus and variety and encouragement and a shared larger vision. But in my present way of life, Lord God, I feel suffocated, trapped in a small dark room where the air is all but consumed.

And then I turn my eyes to you, Lord Christ:

You gave up the infinite space of eternity,
The shining serenity of heaven;
Surrendered your power, honour and rightful glory
To the crushing finitude of our human life.

O my Lord Christ, for what? for whom?
Yes, Lord, I hear you. For us. For me.

You gave up the lovely companionships of eternity
The totally trusting, totally trustworthy loves of heaven;
Were subject to pettiness, scorn, misunderstanding,
And the limited love your friends could give you
And the humiliating death your enemies planned for you.

Yes, Lord, I hear you. For us. For me.

O my Lord, forgive me. For you took to yourself the tedium and frustration of this ordinary human life of mine, and so lived it that it gave glimpses of the glory and richness of the life within it of heaven, for which we were created and for which I so long. You showed how that life of heaven was present to be lived here and now; and you opened up for us the way to do it.

O Lord, help me to grasp hold of that truth today, so that the ordinary things I do and my every encounter, reflect however dimly the lambency of heaven. To which heaven bring me in fullness, my dear Lord Christ, one day. Amen.

PRAYER NOTES

Fifteenth Day · EVENING

> God, in you have I trusted
> Upon you I cast my care;
> Even on you I throw my soul,
> Receive me as I throw myself upon you . . .
>> Keep me when I sleep
>> help me in whatever I do,
> Inspire in me whatever I think
> You, Lord, by your grace. Amen
>
> *Anselm of Canterbury*[26]

O gracious God, I think tonight of all the men and women in whose succession I am, who through the centuries have turned to you as night falls and surrendered themselves afresh to your grace and care. I think particularly of ____ and ____ to whom I owe so much of my faith. Thank you for the inheritance they have left for us of their dialogue with you. Thank you that you answered them in their need and kept them in a faith they were able to pass on to us, enriched by their own living. May it be so for me and my generation, too, Lord.

And now, Father, I make this prayer of Anselm my own. Help me to the same abandonment of self, flinging myself on you in total trust. Let me make the effort of longing and will to 'throw' myself across the gap of doubts and weariness, across the divide created by our present culture, across the chasm of my own failures and miseries, successes and joys, into the warm security of your grasp. Like a parent opening arms wide to the child, catch me, Father, as I make that leap of faith. And so keep me while I sleep, and be with me in my waking, that all I do and am, all I think and feel, all I want and take, is inspired by you. By you, Lord, in your grace. Amen.

PRAYER NOTES

Sixteenth Day · MORNING

Lord, I have made a quiet room in my heart; let the hush of your presence fall on me now.

O, Lord God, the refreshment of looking away from myself to you! I adore you. I praise you. I thank you. I revel in your serenity; your joy; your wisdom; your beauty; your power and purpose; your truth; your holiness; your final gathering up of all. May the wonder of these become more and more the source of my living and being.

Dear Lord, forgive me that daily so much of my prayer is concerned with myself. I so want peace of mind, and health of body, and satisfactory relationships. And so that is what I pray about. But forgive me, Father, when because of this I make you the means and myself the end.

I know it will take a long time and much effort and your divine patience, for me to be weaned from this persistent self-concern, but help me, O God, to go on working at it, for hell can be nothing else but a life of which self is the centre.

And I lift up my heart, O God, for all who, at the mercy of their anxieties, cannot, however they try, wrench their minds from themselves; for whom every demand creates foreboding, the feeling that they cannot cope with all that is required of them.

Confirm in them, dear Lord, the hope that there is a way through this dark valley, and light at the end of it. So lead them to those who can help them, Father. Comfort them and give them courage to face each day, and rest their minds in the certainty that you will see them through.

So, as I leave this room of quiet, lead me in your way for me, and let the certainty of your love take away my fears. So let me, rising up now, follow you. Amen.

Leslie Weatherhead (freely adapted)[27]

PRAYER NOTES

Sixteenth Day · EVENING

Lord,
teach me to rest in you.
Teach me to see the sky
and to think of nothing else
but the joy of it.
Teach me to look
at field and flower
and be soothed
by colours and seasons.
Teach me to close my eyes
and to rest
in the Love that has supported me
all my days.
Teach me, Lord,
to rest in you.

Frank Topping[28]

O Love that has supported all my days, how gratefully I rest tonight in your sure strength. This world is full of colour and light, but my eyes are darkened with weariness. Now as I rest in you, let me recall in my mind's eye your gifts of far horizons and skies that speak of the joys of your love's infinite span. Now as I rest in you let me remember the rooms I have been in today, and everything in them, however small and unpretentious, which offered colour and beauty. Now as I rest in you, recall to me the glimpses I have had of the natural world and its seasons, even in this urban landscape: the skies above the rooftops, the bushes at the corner, the patches of grass, and the trees I pass, the flowers in that window, the sun slanting through the glass, and that flurry of rain with its clear droplets running down the pane.

So, Lord, create in me that deep thankfulness in which I rest my whole world, and especially those I most love, in complete trust, on your love. Amen.

PRAYER NOTES

Seventeenth Day · MORNING

Surrender your rights
to another.
Surrender your rights
to the other

Whether friend or foe
let them go
Christ is always
the other.
Esther de Waal[29]

Lord Christ, I cannot do it. I'm not even sure I ought to try. What about my proper self-respect? What about the integrity of my position? What about the exercise of right judgement, and the vindication of truth? Bluntly, Lord, how can it be right that those others *get away with it*?

No, Lord, I don't exactly want to call down fire from heaven on them. I do remember what you said to your disciples about that. It's just that if my rights are real (and I know that in you they are, because you are God of justice) then how can I properly let them be trampled on?

O my dear Lord, even as I protest I see the answer in your face and in your bleeding body. It's not the justice of the case, is it, Lord, but the mercy? Your mercy? It's thinking with a faint, faint shadow of your marvellously generous love about every being with whom I share the world, even if they are standing offensively on my patch. O Jesus, how can I begin to grasp your kind of loving? that concedes the demand, for love of the person making it. Your kind of loving that even abandoned heaven, your rightful place, so that we might share it with you.

So enlarge my heart, Lord, that I may truly begin to see others that way: as beings whose 'rights' I care for, even at the expense of my own. Let me see you, Christ, in each of them, beginning today. Amen.

PRAYER NOTES

Seventeenth Day · EVENING

O Lord God, thank you for all those who through their wisdom have helped to guide my way today. Thank you for men and women through whom you are speaking in our generation; not only the leaders, but the thousands of ordinary folk who trust you and live lives of obedience and love which honour you and serve your world. Thank you for the wisdom and moral understanding you give through them in these times of shifting values. And help us as a nation to hear them, Lord, and not let their voices be drowned by the brittle cleverness of fashionable personalities, or the seductive voices of those whose restlessness itches always for some new thing.

Tonight, Father, I pray:

— for all the leaders of the churches of this nation; strengthen them with the power that is of your Spirit, and solace them with the peace that only you can give;

— for all who are ordained, or seeking ordination; that in their vocation to be truly servants, you will sustain in them the strength to set aside as a sacrifice every instinct for status or gain which would diminish the clarity, truth, and power, with which they proclaim in their lives as in their words your tender love for all your creatures. And may they know the lovely rewards of your service, Lord;

— for all lay Christians, that you will challenge them to hallow all their work and leisure through their faith; that men and women may recognize in them that they have been with Jesus. Teach them how to speak wisely of your grace that is in them, and so declare, by their living and their being, their speech and their silence, your rule over all things.

And thank you for the gift of your holy church, Lord, through time and space. Forgive us, as a church, our many failures to know your grace and declare it in our manner of life and our institutions. Keep us thankful that nevertheless your Word has been declared through the ages, and we have received it. May our successors know the same gift. Amen.

PRAYER NOTES

Eighteenth Day · MORNING

Jesus confirm my heart's desire
To work and speak and think for Thee
Still let me guard the holy fire
And still stir up the gift in me.
Charles Wesley[30]

O Lord God, you are Lord of this new day of my life. In it I know time and eternity will intertwine in the steady outworking of your kingdom. And yet, Father, so often the eternal things seem remote to me, and the everyday things so much more real. I am seduced by dailiness, Lord; by absorption in all the ordinary demands of living.

Forgive me, Lord, for I know you have called me, and shown me how your grace is present in all that I meet; you have invited me to share that with others. Lord, thank you for the wonder of that calling; in my heart I know my deepest longing is to work and speak and think for you. So I ask:

— that you will forgive the complacency, laziness, inertia or self-centredness which so often and so easily deflects me from your purposes;
— that you will kindle in me continually that fire of love for you, and longing that others may know you, which so often I let burn low;
— that you will inspire in me a joy in all those I meet today; a dedication for your sake to the tasks I must do today; and a faith in your power that confronts all that would dismay or overcome me today.

Lord, in preparation for this day I have spent the night in rest. Bless all those who have spent the night maintaining our security while we slept. Bless all those who have spent the night caring for the sick and dying. Bless all those who in the night have struggled with their own pain and sickness; all those who have watched the long hours in bereavement or perplexity or suspense. Bless all those who did not want the dawn to come; and all who for whatever reason face this morning light wearily. O Christ of Gethsemane, who anguished through the night watches, give them comfort, strength and peace today in body, mind and soul. Amen.

PRAYER NOTES

Eighteenth Day · EVENING

What if the present were the world's last night?
Mark in thy heart, O Soul, where thou dost dwell,
The picture of Christ crucified, and tell
Whether that countenance can thee afright?

John Donne[31]

O God, you are Lord of the night as well as the day, Lord of
all that I fear most, as well as of what I delight in. Now as the
day ends, I bring to you my own and the world's anxieties and
fears. And particularly tonight those latent fears, in our
twentieth-century world, of the final catastrophe. Lord, we
love in such unstable times, with violence and national hatred
widespread across the earth. And the powers for destruction
we now hold are so terrible. We know we have the capacity to
destroy ourselves; and we know that there is that among us
which would do so without compunction.

Lord of all history, Lord of eternity, when such fears assail
me, as they have every generation, help me to turn again to
you in confidence. Thank you for every signal of the power of
your love in lives facing disaster:

— those who speak out fearlessly for truth's sake amidst
double-dealing;
— those who give their energies and risk their lives to give
aid to the victims of war, earthquake, famine and
disease.
— those who give out of small incomes and hard lives to
maintain the charities which offer care to the world's
vulnerable.

Lord, bless, strengthen and encourage them.

And most of all, Lord God and Father, I thank you that you
have underwritten for us the certainties of eternity in the love
of your Son, Jesus Christ. I thank you that the face of God in

history and eternity, the face of the Lord of the last things and the end time, is the compassionate and wholly understanding face of my Lord who gave his life for me. It is the joyful and tender face of my Lord who defeated death for me, comforting his disciples in an upper room. It is your face, Lord, radiant and tender and in glorious power, which invites me to trust in heaven beyond, as well as the heavenly here. Lord, I believe; help all my unbelief! Amen.

PRAYER NOTES

Nineteenth Day · MORNING

'Lord, to whom else can we go? you have the words of
life . . .'

John 6.68

O Lord God of the universe, thank you that this morning is
not simply an arbitrary unit in a random sequence of days.
Thank you that there is design, purpose and order in your
universe, because you have made it so. Thank you that there is
design, order and purpose in human life because you have
willed it so. Thank you that there is design, order and purpose
inherent in whatever happens to me today, because such is
your nature and your plan for me. So, Lord, I ask you to make
yourself known today to:

- all who truly seek for a meaning in life;
- all who fear that life is random;
- all whose calling is to study and expound matters of
  philosophy, ethics and theology;
- all who through the arts or the media affect others'
  understanding of life.

Especially, Lord, I think of ____ and ____.

And, Lord, begin with me, that my own understanding may
always be open to your greater and more profound truth; that
my heart may always be open to your greater, more searching
love; that my spirit may always be open to greater awe of your
holiness.

And in your love and compassion, Father, encounter and
irradiate all those whose experience of life has so hurt or
maimed them, or so disillusioned or deadened their spirits
that no words of life have any meaning for them.

May they meet you on their journey, and find in you hope

and significance. In the name of Christ, whose words are life.
Amen.

PRAYER NOTES

I believe that God is real
Even though I cannot realize him;
That what I commit to him, he will glorify,
  and use for his eternal purpose.
I believe that his will is love to all of us
His ways are not our ways,
But we may come to him
  Through Jesus,
  Through his Spirit,
Through all beauty, love and truth.

Margaret Cropper[32]

I believe that God is real: O God, all day you have seemed so far off; and unreal; it has been so tempting to live as though you were not. In this time of quiet, Lord, help me to accept in an act of faith that sense of remoteness: and to affirm what I *know*, even when I cannot *feel*:

'I believe that God is real.'

I believe he will glorify what I commit to him: O God, all day it has felt as though there was no guidance for me in my doing and being, even though I longed for it. In this time of quiet, Lord, help me to trust that thoughts, words and deeds which were truly offered to you will be directed and their intention honoured: and that you will use them in your mighty purposes.

I believe he will receive and use to
his glory what I commit to him.

I believe that his will is love to all: O God, sometimes it is so difficult to go on being sure that love is the law of the universe. The suffering and misery you allow seem love's very reverse. You ask your friends, Lord, to accept such hardness as no human friendship would require. In this time of quiet, Lord, help me, help me to affirm whilst your purpose is opaque and your love to us all obscured, what I know in moments of closeness to you, in moments of seeing, in moments of understanding:

what I know when I look at Jesus;
what I know when the Spirit speaks;
what I have seen in the beauty, truth and love present even in the worst periods of human life.

I believe your will, O God, is love to all of us. Amen.

PRAYER NOTES

Twentieth Day · MORNING

And we hear them telling in our own
tongues the mighty works of God.

Acts 2.11 RSV

O Lord God Almighty, as I go out to this day's living I am
seized with a strong sense of thankfulness and awe at your
mighty works in this world and in my life.

The physical universes in all their mystery and order, design, intricacy and beauty, vast still beyond our measuring:
these are your mighty works.

— *I praise and glorify you, O God.*

The interior universe of the human spirit, its mysteriousness
and lucidity, passion and intricacy, vision and practicality,
idealism and grief, instinct for beauty and capacity for desola-
tion, vast still beyond measuring: these are your mighty
works.

— *I praise and glorify you, O God.*

This beautiful planet earth, with its seas and continents,
mountains, plains, deserts and rainforests, creatures and
plants, vast resources of rock depth and sea depths still
beyond our measuring: these are your mighty works.

— *I praise and glorify you, O God.*

This life you have given me, this day before me: with its
hopes and fears, its human encounters, its loves and friend-
ships, its antagonisms and hurts, its anger and its joy, its
tedium and its pleasures, its delight in your love and the challenge and joy of your service: vast possibilities of heavenly
life, here and to come, still beyond my measuring: these too
are your mighty works.

— *I praise and glorify you, O God.*

O Lord God, whose people, inspired by your Spirit, first told out your mighty works, the ultimate victory of your good over every power of evil and destruction: may my voice be joined to theirs, so that others in my own generation may hear me, too, telling in their own tongue of your mighty works. Amen.

PRAYER NOTES

Twentieth Day · EVENING

Some ask the world
  and are diminished
in the receiving
  of it. You give me

only this small pool
  that the more I drink
from, the more overflows
  me with sourceless light.
                              R. S. Thomas[33]

Lord, I look back in wonder. Often I wanted something bigger or more dramatic or more world-challenging than you seemed to be permitting; and yet in this small pool where you have set me I have become increasingly aware of the depth and richness of your love for your whole creation. The world is full of small places where you have worked your will: Bethlehem, Nazareth, Cana, Capernaum, Assisi, Lourdes, Canterbury, Iona . . . and this street, this corner where I live. So tonight let me affirm with thankfulness the marvellous truth that your light haloes the most ordinary lives and situations; and heaven lies all around me where I live.

Tonight, Father, I thank you:

— for the ordinary exchanges of life among my family and loved ones, for the home in which you have been with us, and for our shared life;
— for the unpraised tasks done by others all round me, for the patience and kindness of those who take time and trouble for others, often when weary themselves. Forgive me that I have myself so often failed in such generosity.

O Lord Christ, who chose to make yourself known in a small and unimportant place, make yourself known in my heart tonight, and teach me to drink contentedly and trustingly of your overflowing sourceless light, from the small pool by which you have set me. Amen.

~

PRAYER NOTES

Twenty-first Day · MORNING

The trivial round, the common task,
Will furnish all I need to ask;
Room to deny ourselves, a road
To bring us daily nearer God.

Only, O Lord, in thy dear love
Fit us for perfect rest above;
And help us this and every day
To live more nearly as we pray.
John Keble [34]

O my dear Lord, mighty God, Creator of all that is, I long to break through the boundaries of what I can see and know of you, I long for high revelation, I long for a noble task to do for you and the loftiness of vision that goes with it. Instead here I am, Lord, facing another grey and ordinary day with its routine and tedium and its pettinesses.

How can I learn of you, high and holy God, and serve you rightly, in the midst of domesticity and dailiness? How can I ever find freedom from the tyranny of little things and small demands to talk with you, Lord, as I should? The incessant demands of the younger members of the family, Lord, the knocks on the door, the telephone, the things that go wrong in the house, the time and energy everything takes just to sustain the ordinariness of living: there is no energy to make any offering of life worthy of you . . .

Help me, my dear Lord, to accept the truth I want to refuse. I thought discipleship ought to be a glorious calling: and this feels so mundane. But then I look at you, my Lord Jesus, living so ordinarily for thirty years; and I know that 'ordinary' time was of a piece with your glorious public ministry.

O Lord my God, help me translate my longing to serve you greatly into those acts of loving self-denial needed hourly in the ordinariness of life; and let me understand the wonder, that such small denying of self is of a piece with the Lord Jesus picking up the heavy wooden cross. So may I be brought daily nearer you, and fitted as may best be for the life of heaven, now and forever. Amen.

PRAYER NOTES

Twenty-first Day · EVENING

Tonight, Lord, as I look back over the day, I re-affirm that the world is yours, and all in it. So I ask, what has that meant in practical terms for my care of others? And I ponder the Iona hymn:[35]

> Christ's is the world in which we move,
> Christ's are the folk we're summoned to love,
> Christ's is the voice which calls us to care,
> And Christ is the one who meets us here.

So did I, today,

> Feel for the people we most avoid,
> Strange or bereaved or never employed;
> Feel for the women and feel for the men
> Who fear that their living is all in vain.

> *Lord, here and now I think of them,*
> *take them on my heart and pray for them.*

So did I, today,

> Feel for the parents who've lost their child
> Feel for the women whom men have defiled,
> Feel for the baby for whom there's no breast
> And feel for the weary who find no rest.

> *Lord, here and now I think of them,*
> *take them on my heart and pray for them.*

So did I, today,

> Feel for the lives by life confused,
> Riddled with doubt, in loving abused;
> Feel for the lonely heart, conscious of sin,
> Which longs to be pure but fears to begin.

Lord, here and now I think of them,
take them on my heart and pray for them.

To the lost, Christ shows his face;
To the unloved he gives his embrace;
To those who cry, in pain or disgrace
Christ makes, with his friends, a touching place.

Filled with compassion, Jesus reached out his hand and touched the leper . . .

O Christ, forgive what I have not felt; and so enlarge my heart that I never shrink from contact with your loved ones who are the world's rejects. Instead, teach me to love and care rightly, in your name. Amen.

PRAYER NOTES

Twenty-second Day · MORNING

> Lord, you came to give us life,
> and life that was more abundant.
> Help me not to run away from life
> but to follow your spirit,
> to accept the thorn
> as well as the flower,
> and to be grateful
> for the gift of life.
>
> *Frank Topping*[36]

O God, Father of us all, I so often begin these mornings full of hope and commitment, ready to see you in all I encounter, and there live for you. And then, Lord, I am bruised by the hard realities of life which are so different from the morning vision. I go out towards people looking to all that may be good and fruitful between us: and often I simply meet cynicism, selfishness, suspicion, scorn, mockery or just plain lack of understanding, or misinterpretation. My words are misplaced or mis-heard; my actions seem ineffective or inappropriate, too urgent or too radical or too little or too late, or based on a rejected set of values.

And I long to run away, Father. To close myself off from these harsh encounters, this wasted expenditure of spirit.

O my loving Father, help me to accept and love as part of the wholeness of your world, the thorn as well as the flower. Help me to value and treasure not some idealized version of life, but life itself, in its hardness as well as its gentleness. Help me to respect and honour all those among whom I live, not as they conform to some image I project, but in all their variousness.

So this morning, Lord, I thank you for all the seasons, winter and summer, cold and heat; for all your creatures, predatory and domestic, the ugly and the beautiful; for the marvellous variety of humankind; for the distinctive gifts of each individual; for the particular characteristics of each community.

O Lord, help me more and more to grow into Christ's way of loving, who never imposed uniformity, but redeemed particularity. Let me rejoice in all that is to me different and alien, and yet baptized in your grace. So let me revel in your gift of life in its abundance, Lord. Amen.

———

PRAYER NOTES

Twenty-second Day · EVENING

Leave it all quietly to God, my soul, my rescue comes
from him alone.

Psalm 62, (trans. Moffat)

O my Lord God, I sometimes feel so sick at heart over the
images I see on my television screen, or at what I read in the
newspapers or hear on the radio. My world seems so sick,
Lord, and I so helpless.

O my God, I bring to you the horror of the fanatical national-
ism that sweeps across the world, the ethnic hatreds and the
terrible brutality that supports them. Judge and Saviour, bless
and strengthen as you have in the past, all who challenge wrong-
ful pride among nations; all who seek to alleviate the suffering it
causes; all who work to protect weaker racial groups; all who
struggle to bring about honourable peace.

And, Lord God, help me not to leave this to others, but, by
what I say and do and am, to share the struggle, speak the
truth, and carry in my heart grief for the suffering.

O my God, I bring to you the disarray of my own nation,
our gathering violence, our promiscuity, our selfishness, our
failure to live up to the ideals we publicly proclaim, and above
all our national loss of knowledge of you, and our moral
confusion. Judge and Saviour, bless and strengthen as you
have in the past, all who work to protect the vulnerable, all
who seek to control and assuage violence, all who challenge
selfishness as an acceptable philosophy of life, all who work
to redeem the political life of the country, all who seek by
word and deed to share you with a nation which largely does
not know you.

And, Lord God, help me not to leave this to others, but, by
what I do and say and am, to share the struggle, grieve with
those who suffer or are near despair and speak out not only
your truth but your love.

Dear Lord, when I ponder these things I am shaken by distress and frustration. Help me to use all my best energies in the fight against the corrosion of your world; and having done so, to rest my soul quietly in trust that the outcome is in your hands: and I may safely leave it there. Amen.

PRAYER NOTES

Twenty-third Day · MORNING

> Lord, teach me the art of patience whilst I am well, and
> give me the use of it when I am sick. In that day either
> lighten my burden or strengthen my back. Make me who
> so often in my health have discovered my weakness
> presuming on my own strength, to be strong in my
> sickness when I solely rely on Thy assistance.
>
> *Thomas Fuller*[37]

O Lord God, I so savour the joys of health and vigour; life is
so full of things to do and people to meet, and I so rarely
stop to recognize how much of all that variety and richness is
available to me because of my good health. But all around
me there are those whose sickness, age or disability cut them
off from so much that fills my life and gives me pleasure. Yet
so many of them are brimming with a different kind of richness, Lord; they are people I want to spend time with for my
own sake, because of the quality of their being, their insights
and their understanding. And their patience, Lord . . . When
they speak of you I am a child learning from the truly grown-
up in Christ. I thank you for them, I ask your continued
enrichment of them. I think especially of ____ and ____.

So, Lord, help me to make this prayer of Thomas Fuller's
my own. Teach me, today and in the coming days, the art of
your patience, now, whilst I am fit and able. I think of the
patience with which you endured the Cross, Lord; and of how
that was nourished and practised in Galilee and Jerusalem,
with your disciples, with your opponents, with the crowds. So
help me to nourish and practise that same patience in my
active life now, Lord: that it may be available for whatever
purposes you will, in future stages of my life.

And when illness or age slacken my step and slow my energies, then help me to be quietly patient with myself, strong in
patience for others, and cheerfully patient in waiting for you,

to lighten my load or strengthen my back. For your name's sake. Amen.

PRAYER NOTES

Lord God, thank you for the prayers handed down to us by your faithful men and women of the past. Help me to learn from them the marvels of love and faithfulness and generosity and holiness which ordinary human beings have shown when their total trust is in you. O Lord, nurture my spirit by whatever means are necessary, to the kind of Christ-like understanding of your love, and living by it, which enabled this prayer to be written amid the horrors of Ravensbruck:[38]

O Lord, remember not only the men and women of good will, but also those of ill will. But do not remember all the suffering they have inflicted on us; remember the fruits we have bought, thanks to this suffering — our comradeship, our loyalty, our humility, our courage, our generosity, the greatness of heart which has grown out of all this; and when they come to judgement let all the fruits which we have borne be their forgiveness.

O Lord, when I fear for myself or loved ones the threat of others' violence or greed, or fanatical desire for power, bring to my mind those who have suffered the darkest horrors at the hands of others, and have conquered, in your power, both fear and bitterness.

O Lord, when I react to slights and minor injuries as though they were deadly and unassuagable wounds, bring to my mind those who have suffered the darkest horrors at the hands of others, and have conquered, in your power, both fear and bitterness.

O Lord, when in anger I cannot pray for those who have acted or spoken as though they were enemies to me, bring to my mind those who have suffered the darkest horrors at the hands of others, and have conquered in your power both fear and bitterness.

O Lord, let me look away from myself and my fears and resentments to the wonder of what you can do with human lives, and the fruits you can nurture in them even in vile places. So may I not so much lament the wickedness of which we are capable as marvel at the goodness you can create in us. May it be so in my life, Lord. Amen.

PRAYER NOTES

Twenty-fourth Day · MORNING

The Wire Fence

The wires are holding hands around the holes:
To avoid breaking the ring, they hold tight
   the neighbouring wrist,
And it's thus that with holes they make a fence.

Lord, there are lots of holes in my life.
There are some in the lives of my neighbours.
But if you wish we shall hold hands
We shall hold very tight
And together we shall make a fine roll of
   fence to adorn Paradise.

Michel Quoist[39]

Lord, help me today to see the 'holes in my life' in this fruitful way, so that even my lack can be to your glory. O Father God, praise be to you that when I try to be self-sufficient the gaps in my life make me fail; but when I see myself as one with my neighbours, my life closely entwined with theirs, then together we create something of usefulness and beauty, an offering for Paradise.

So today, Lord, accept my life with all its gaps, and teach me so to share in the life of my neighbours that our weaknesses become a strength for you. In Christ's name. Amen.

PRAYER NOTES

Twenty-fourth Day · EVENING

O Creator Lord, high and holy God, all-seeing Judge, tender Father, you create and sustain all things; and by your will I, too, have my being. So as my day ends, I turn to you, Lord God, for refreshment and strength in thinking of you.

Creator Lord, you are the source of all the delight we have in making: the artist's struggle and joy; the builder's design and strength; the broderer's delicacy and patience; the writer's accuracy and vision; the homemaker's care and order; the musician's touch and sensitivity; the struggle each of us knows to draw out of the chaos of each day's life, harmony and order.

> *All these are signs of what you are, my Lord God: in you I delight, in you I rest.*

High and holy God, you are the source of all our sense of reverence, our awe before the holy, our instinct that beyond the reach of reason there is mystery. It is you who inspires in us a longing for purity, for integrity; and a hatred of all that corrupts or despoils. You teach us that far, far beyond human vision and aspiration is an intensity of light, harmony and beauty which is the language of your purity: and you inspire in us a longing for it. You are the source and end of that sense of worship which unites those of us who love you, Lord.

> *All these are signs of what you are, my Lord God: in you I delight, in you I rest.*

All-seeing Judge, you are the source of our sense that wrong matters and good must prevail. You inspire within us aspirations to justice and fairness. You are the victims' defence in the struggle against aggression and extortion. You undergird those who seek to bring hidden evil to light, to vindicate the innocent. You are there in our collective anger against those who hurt or destroy little children; you are there in an individual's unpopular and lonely fight for justice.

All these are signs of what you are, my Lord God: in you I delight, in you I rest.

O my *tender Father*, you are all these, but most of all you are Love. So in you I delight, and delighting, take my rest. Amen.

~

PRAYER NOTES

Twenty-fifth Day · MORNING

O Lord my God, this day is yours; therefore let my journey through it be one of learning from you. And to help me, may I make my own this prayer from John Baillie:

> Teach me . . . so to use all the circumstances of my life today that they may bring forth in me the fruits of holiness rather than the fruits of sin:
>
> Let me use disappointment as material for
>   patience:
> Let me use success as material for thanks-
>   giving:
> Let me use suspense as material for
>   perseverance:
> Let me use danger as material for courage:
> Let me use reproach as material for long-
>   suffering:
> Let me use praise as material for humility:
> Let me use pleasure as material for
>   temperance:
> Let me use pains as material for endurance.

John Baillie[40]

But, my dear Lord, do not let all this lead me merely into self-concern and anxious self-examination. Lead me instead into that way of holiness which looks always away from itself to you and your tender love for the world. So may I be strengthened against selfishness, and drawn into sharing with you in service to, and care of, your people. May I grow in patience, thankfulness, perseverance, courage, long-suffering, humility, temperance and endurance, because I am rooted and grounded in your love, and patterned on your life. So bring me to the foot of the Cross, Lord. Amen.

PRAYER NOTES

Twenty-fifth Day · EVENING

'Thou shalt not be overcome' was said full clearly . . . he said not 'Thou shalt not be tempested, thou shalt not be travailed, thou shalt not be dis-eased', but he said 'Thou shalt not be overcome'.

Julian of Norwich[41]

O gracious and sustaining Lord, I rest tonight on the wonder and comfort of this promise. Sometimes life is so frightening, Lord: not simply its circumstances, but what those do to our inner selves, the ways in which who and what we truly are can be threatened with distortion, or stunting, by the battering of tragedy in our lives. Or we can be so overspent in the demands of relationships or activities or sheer hard labour, that the space within the heart we need to be our true selves is diminished almost to nothing. Or our lives are so empty, so underemployed, so unvalued by others, so lacking in love or in imaginative or emotional or spiritual life of any kind, that our inner selves fade to mere wisps, faint shadows of the living souls they should be.

Lord, I am conscious that I have myself only walked on the edge of such experiences. But even only ankle-deep was frightening; and to see others threatened, tempested, dis-eased, travailed, sears my heart with grief for them and fear for me and mine. So tonight I rest on this promise, Lord. You have made, and you will bear: and though life's circumstances may stun me, batter me, exhaust me, terrify me, yet you have promised to sustain me, the inner me which you have made for eternity.

So in the name and power of my Lord Jesus Christ, who walked the fells of horror and death and was not overcome, I pray that I too may not be overcome, even by fears that I *shall* be overcome. Instead let me turn to you in confidence in all circumstances, for meaning, strength, and space for my soul to grow towards your light. Amen.

~

PRAYER NOTES

Twenty-sixth Day · MORNING

Lord, my sins: personal and collective:

> The sins of the world,
> such dreadful sins,
> not just the personal sins
> but the solidarity of sin
> greater than the total
>   of individual sins,
> nuclear evil in endless fission,
>   O Lamb of God.
>
> The sin of racial pride
> that sees not the faith
>   that all men are divinely made . . .
> that each is the sibling
>   for whom Christ died.
>
> The burgeoning greed
>   that never heeds the needs of others
> involved in a merciless system,
> looking only at profit and dividend,
> the lust of possessions
>   that cannot accompany us
>   at our last migration.
> Take away these sins,
>   O Lamb of God.
>
> The massive sin of war . . .
> billions of pounds wasted
>   on weapons, bombs . . .
>   the hungry still unfed,
>   grief stalking unnumbered homes:
> Weep over us,
> O Lamb of God.

The sin of the world,
   alienation from thee
   not just weakness
   but evil intention . . .
O Lamb of God
   take away this sin.

Begin with me,
O Lamb of God,
   forgive my sins,
   cleanse my heart,
   disarm my will
   and let me fight
   armed with thy truth, righteousness and love
   with thy cross of love
   incised upon my heart,
O Lamb of God.

George Appleton (adapted)[42]

～

PRAYER NOTES

Twenty-sixth Day · EVENING

Save us while waking, and guard us while sleeping; that awake we may watch with Christ, and asleep we may rest in peace.

Antiphon, Service of Compline

O most gracious and loving God, all the hours are yours and all that I do in them. So tonight I bring to you all my watching with you through the daylight hours; and I ask your peace for the night ahead.

Lord, I ask you to save me from either complacency or self-doubt as I look back over the day: help me now in this time of reflection to judge rightly, and acknowledge honestly to you, what in my doing or saying or bearing was under your authority, and what in them ignored or denied you.

Loving Lord, forgive me, save me, bless me.

Lord, I ask you to save me from either apprehension or facile ease of mind as I think of tomorrow. Help me now to offer to your safe keeping all that I know lies before me, all that I fear, and all that I hope; all I need to prepare myself for, and all that may be unexpected which I cannot prepare for. Keep me honest and un-evasive in the face of anything which comes to me as a consequence of former wrong-doing. Keep me steady and humble at anything which comes to me as a consequence of some former good I have done. Whether I am full or empty, may tomorrow also be a day of watching with Christ.

Loving Lord, forgive me, save me, bless me.

So, Lord, quiet my thoughts now in the profound safety of your love. If I cannot sleep, help me to centre my wandering thoughts on your goodness. And guard my undefended soul in slumber, that my dreams are under your control, and I fear neither sleeping nor waking. Amen.

PRAYER NOTES

Twenty-seventh Day · MORNING

> On the estate, lord, the people
> Take counsel one with another
> And in the public house
> There is lamentation.
> The cost of living soars
> Like wild ducks rising
> After morning feed.
> Man has neither means nor meaning.
> The cry of the young in the street
> Rouses a protest in the market place.
> What shall I do, Lord?
>
> *Cliff Ashby*[43]

What shall I do? O Lord, what shall I do? in lives all around me in this city it is so clear that 'man has neither means nor meaning'. There is such hardship, Lord, such grey misery shot with fear in so many of our vandalized estates; and yet such talent and energy, dribbling away in unemployment and boredom and crime and hopelessness. The public houses give rituals of shared anxieties and brief and facile fellowship; but means and meaning are not their business. And the young, Lord; so many of them disillusioned or cynical or angry. They want to be valued. They want a chance to live; really to live: not simply to exist. Where is there means and meaning for them? What shall I do, Lord?

I look for you, Lord, and I find you on the estate itself, at its centre. You were homeless, born in a sort of cardboard city. The police sought you. You grew up among an oppressed people in an occupied country; you knew its anger, you knew its poverty, you knew its fear of loss of meaning and its widespread lack of means.

So this estate is yours, Lord, and its people. And that must mean it's mine, too. Help me to own it. To do what I can —

politically, socially, economically, to 'own' it as mine. Help me to care about the tired struggles of its old people, and the angry bravado of its youth. Help me to declare by deed as well as word that there is meaning to life on the estate, and it is God's meaning; that there are the national means to create life there as it should be, and that God requires us to use them.

And help me to proclaim that it is *your* means and *your* meaning that gives hope to the estate. That is what I shall do, Lord. Amen.

~

PRAYER NOTES

Twenty-seventh Day · EVENING

God help my thoughts! they stray from me,
    setting off on the wildest journeys;
When I am at prayer, they run off like
    naughty children, quarrelling, making
    trouble.
When I read the Bible, they fly to a distant
    place, filled with seductions.
My thoughts can cross an ocean with a single
    leap; they can fly from earth to heaven,
    and back again, in a single second.
They come to me for a fleeting moment, and
    then away they flee. No chains, no locks
    can hold them back; no threats of
    punishment can restrain them, no hiss
    of a lash can frighten them.
They slip from my grasp like tails of eels;
    they swoop hither and thither like swallows
    in flight.
Dear, chaste Christ, who can see into every
    heart, and read every mind, take hold of my
    thoughts. Bring my thoughts back to me,
    and clasp me to yourself. Amen.

Celtic Prayers[44]

So, Father, quiet me as a child is quieted; so that I may offer this day's living to you trustfully, filled only with the thought of your loving-kindness as you receive it.

Forgive all wrong in it, Father, and bless all that has been good. And let me keep heart and thought fixed on you as I ask this: do not let my soul be caught in the slipstream of my own doings and thinkings.

Be with those tonight suffering stress or agitation or pain; and strengthen and support all those working for their relief.

And increase in us all a singlemindedness in your love; that all our wanderings of body, mind and spirit are finally gathered up into the homecoming of your heaven. Through Christ our Lord. Amen.

〜

PRAYER NOTES

Twenty-eighth Day · MORNING

> O God, the problem with my anger unleashed
> is the same as that of my love tied up.
> It puts me at the centre
> and is the greatest idolatry.
>
> *Kathy Galloway*[45]

O my Lord, I cannot rest tonight because of my anger. And yet, Lord, I do not know how to be angry without sinning. Teach me, when:

— I am angry with those who have the means and the authority to alleviate poverty and homelessness, and do not do it;

— I am angry with those in your church who seem to care more for observances than for the proclamation of your astounding love;

— I am angry with politicians who spend their skill on clever political manipulation instead of risking their position to resolve hard issues;

— I am angry with those I live among who do not carry their share of the load, or seem not to value me;

— sometimes, Lord, I am even angry with the weather!

O my Lord, I discern in my anger a sense of self-righteousness which is much too close to pleasure. And I think of you, Lord. You were never angry in your own defence, and you took no pleasure in anger: else why the Cross? But you were angry for God: you were angry with those who sold him as a commodity; you were angry with those who used him for their own status; or who treated him as belonging only to them.

O Lord, implant in me a holy fear of the wrong kind of anger, which ministers to my own sense of self-importance, or is simply an indulgence of my own frustration. Forgive me, Lord, for all such occasions: I think particularly of ____ and ____.

O Lord, keep me in awe of your holy anger, and let me never seek to counterfeit it. Forgive me, Lord, for all such occasions: I think particularly of ____ and ____.

And Lord, let me live so close to you that should that rare moment come when I must speak out with your anger against the unholy, I may do so with conviction, selflessness and power. To the glory of God the Father. Amen.

~

PRAYER NOTES

Twenty-eighth Day · EVENING

Were you there when they crucified my Lord?
Were you there? . . .
O sometimes it causes me to tremble, tremble,
  tremble,
Were you there when they crucified my Lord?
Traditional Spiritual

Lord, was I there?
Am I there among your disciples who flee? In the face of threat
or mockery or humiliation, am I among those who back down
from my belief or deny my friendship or run away?

Sometimes, Lord, it causes me to tremble, tremble, tremble . . .

Lord, was I there?
When they drag you through the city, am I there? One of an
unthinking crowd, seeking entertainment, thoughtless and heart-
less? Or judging or persecuting someone whom the group has
made a victim, or silent while others do? Assenting to the major-
ity view, rather than going by conscience? Am I there, Lord?

Sometimes, Lord, it causes me to tremble, tremble, tremble . . .

Lord, was I there?
In that pharisaical group wagging self-righteous heads around
the Cross? Delighting in appropriate retribution rather than
mercy? Just, and pitiless? Lord, am I there?

Sometimes, Lord, it causes me to tremble, tremble, tremble . . .

Lord, was I there?
With those who love you, grieving beneath the Cross? Am I
there? As they support each other, and suffer with you, am I
there? Let me be there, Lord, trembling but there . . .

And may I be there with them, Lord, later: with them in
dawning hope at the empty tomb; with them in astonished joy

in the upper room; with them at Pentecost, crowned in the flame of your Spirit;

O Lord, the hope makes me tremble, tremble, tremble . . . O Lord, may I be there. Amen.

PRAYER NOTES

Twenty-ninth Day · MORNING

O loving Father, make me like Jesus:

The Jesus who could spend nights in prayer;
(Do I? *ever*? half a night? three hours? one?)
The Jesus who went about doing good;
(Is this my chief longing? or a hazy general intention?)
The Jesus who made time to talk to Nicodemus;
(How patiently do I give time to the Nicodemus who wants
to talk? The old lady in the shopping centre? The junior in
the office? The elderly relative in the nursing home? The
teenage children? My spouse? My friend?)
The Jesus who could not bear to see the mother cry at
Nain;
(Do I open myself to other people's grief, Lord? Or refuse
the load on my heart?)
The Jesus who could sleep peacefully in a gale and storm;
(How much is my own faith at the mercy of circumstances,
Lord?)
The Jesus who would not let the marriage at Cana be spoilt
by lack of wine;
(How much, Lord, am I willing to give myself to the ordin-
ary occasions of other people's lives? in time? in energy? in
money? in caring?)
The Jesus who was strong enough not to answer back
when accused unjustly;
(How instinctively defensive am I, Lord, and what do I do
about it?)
The Jesus who could shrink from the cup of suffering, yet
drain it to the last dregs;
(O Lord, certainly I shrink from suffering; keep me more
faithful when required to endure it.)
The Jesus who could pray for the men who nailed him to
the cross;

(O Lord, I do not know how to pray for those who hurt me: but I do know I long to be able to. Teach me, Lord.)

O loving Father, make me like the Jesus who came to the world,
To show what you were like. Amen.

Based on a personal prayer of Bishop Jacob of Travancore, South India.[46]

~

PRAYER NOTES

Twenty-ninth Day · EVENING

The things, good Lord, that I pray for; give me grace to
labour for.

Sir Thomas More[47]

O my loving Father God, to whom I come home in the evening, help me now to look truthfully in your presence at what
I have done and been today:

— Did I live it as a day belonging to you, or did I, perhaps
  unconsciously, take it back?
— Did I evade anything I knew in my heart you wanted
  me to face? Did I move by speech or action in a dir-
  ection I knew in my heart was not your will for me?

> *Help me in your love and mercy to*
> *answer truthfully, dear Lord.*

— Have I been judgemental of others, but self-justifying
  towards myself?
— Have I been your good steward of my time? my energies? my skills? my income? my home? or have I let self-
  indulgence or self-will direct them?
— Have I let 'I want', or 'I have a right to' take charge?

> *Help me in your love and mercy to*
> *answer truthfully, dear Lord.*

— Was I throughout the day aware of, and concerned for,
  others' hopes and burdens and fears and joys?
— Were my eyes open to the world beyond my small concerns? Was my imagination prepared to entertain, even
  where it caused me discomfort or distress, those whose
  style and priorities were alien to me?

> *Help me in your love and mercy to*
> *answer truthfully, dear Lord.*

O Lord, thank you for holding me in your will today: bless and grace all that has been well done in my day, and redeem all that was ill. And with each day that passes may I be delivered, through the power of Jesus Christ, from my besetting sins, my secret and whispering sins, my public and acknowledged sins. So may I lie down to sleep forgiven, affirmed and hopeful, in Jesus Christ. Amen.

~

PRAYER NOTES

Thirtieth Day · MORNING

And all the wickedness in this world —
>   that men might work or think,
Is no more to the mercy of God —
>   than a live coal in the sea.
>   *William Langland*[48]

Lord, I have just been listening to the news on the radio. Sometimes it is hard to believe your justice and truth and mercy and love are still at work, still alive and moving among us. Everywhere there seems discord and greed, the collapse of moral structures and the abandonment of religious faith. And yet I do not know what to believe of what is reported of the world's life, though my own small area of life refracts the general disturbance. We seem at the mercy of manipulation, and your truth is hard to find.

So today I bring to you, dear Lord, this burden of troubled questioning. The news of the day seems to say you are not in charge, Lord. How shall I hold fast to your truth?

And then I think back over the centuries, and recognize that your justice and truth and mercy and love have never been the world's headlines; that always they have been at work secretly, often seen only by the eye of faith. How else could Langland have made his great claim of your victory, in the miseries of his disturbed age, with its brutalities, desperate poverty and Black Death? What were the headlines in Jerusalem, my Lord Christ, the day you were crucified? And on Easter Day, were the headlines of resurrection, of God's great victory over death, or of grave robbers and rumours of ghosts?

O my dear and living Lord, help me not to be seduced into seeing as the world sees, and reporting as the world reports. Help me to see, as your faithful men and women have always seen, that all the wickedness in this world that human beings might work or think, is no more to the mercy of God than a live coal in the sea. So, Lord, whenever the day's news threatens my faith's hold on your victory, help me to hear the hiss of that live coal of wickedness extinguished in the wide seas of your loving mercy. For Jesus' sake. Amen.

PRAYER NOTES

Thirtieth Day · EVENING

Lord, in this blessed quietness, I rest my spirit on these great hymns of your peace:

> Christ, my Beloved, which still doth feed
> Among the flowers, having delight
>   Among his faithful lilies,
> Doth take great care for me indeed
> And I again with all my might
> Will do what so his will is.
>
> My Love in me and I in him,
> Conjoined by love, will still abide
>   Among the faithful lilies
> Till day doth break, and truth do dim
> All shadows dark, and cause them slide
>   According as his will is.
>
>   *William Baldwin*[49]

My God and my Lord, eyes are at rest, stars are setting, hushed are the movements of birds in their nests . . . And thou art the just who knowest no change, the equity that swerveth not, the everlasting that passeth not away. The doors are locked. . . . But thy love is open to him who calls on thee. My Lord, each lover is now alone with his beloved. Thou for me art the beloved One.

                   Abd Ab' Azuz Al-Dirini[50]

May He support us all the day long, till the shades lengthen, and the evening comes, and the busy world is hushed, and the fever of life is over, and our work is done. Then in His mercy may He give us a safe lodging, and a holy rest, and peace at the last. Amen.

                   J. H. Newman[51]

PRAYER NOTES

Thirty-first Day · MORNING

My prayer-bird was cold — would not away,
Although I set it on the edge of the nest.
Then I bethought me of the story old —
Love-fact or loving fable, thou knowest best
How, when the children had made sparrows of
    clay,
Thou mad'st them birds, with wings to
    flutter and fold:
Take, Lord, my prayer in thy hand and make
    it pray.

Based on the story of the child Jesus
in the Apocryphal Gospel of Thomas[52]

Lord God, on this last morning of the month I look back at
the time I have spent in prayer with you, and grieve that it has
been so poor an offering.

So often I have rushed my time with you under the pressure
of other imagined urgencies. So often, even when I have spent
time, my commitment has been shallow and my thoughts
flittering.

So often when I needed you most I have shied away from
meeting your clear, loving gaze. So often I evaded your guidance on things close to my heart; or failed to bring to you
those in need or distress, to whom I owed a debt of prayer; or
tried to hide what I knew in me to be wrong.

So often, above all, I did not simply spend time in the
wonder of adoration and praise and thanksgiving which is my
heart's best and happiest response to your holiness.

Yet, Lord, you know that when I am most true to myself
my heart is hungry for you, longing to offer itself to you,
delighting when it finds you and can nestle in your love. But
so often my prayer-birds will not fly, Lord: without your
blessing, your in-spiration, they are mere clay. As I am. As I

am. So, Lord, take my prayer in your hand and make it pray.
And with it my life: body, mind, heart and soul. And to you be
all praise and glory, all joy and honour. Amen.

PRAYER NOTES

Thirty-first Day · EVENING

O Lord God, as this month ends, I make this version of Psalm 151 my own, in glory to you and with deep thankfulness:

I am come, a long time after the event, to say that *God is Here*;
and not merely in the candlelit places, nor the souls of the inspired, but in this street.
He is running like the winter, like the rain along this street. He is dancing with the leaves in the gutter.
He is in the music of the elderly tramp, blowing and gasping on the wet and windy corner. He is in the bobbing masses moving unconsciously to the rhythm of the music.
He is trembling with the trees, with the sky mirrored in the shop window; he is entwined around the railings of the yard where scrap is sold.
He is hidden in the averted faces of the crowds as they shuffle along the street with down-turned vision. He is the new grass parting the concrete, and the artistry of a snail.
Oh the Lord is in me and may not be measured. Within the convoluted folds of this raincoat, I am extended inwards to all infinity.
In the wet blue darkness the car lamps shine, and are captured by the myriad drops of rain, and the running streams of water on the pavement.
Each lamp reflects the light of the sun, and is in turn reflected by the shop windows, which are reflected in other shop windows, and so on world without end.
So the Lord makes his face to shine upon me, and leads me to the places of light.
Glory be to the stars, and to the beetles, and to his holy substance:
Which, as it was in the beginning, is now and ever shall be.
Olivia Michael[53]

~

PRAYER NOTES

Sunday · MORNING

May none of God's wonderful works
    Keep silence, night or morning.
Bright stars, high mountains, the depths of
    the seas,
        Sources of rushing rivers:
may all these break into song as we sing
    to Father, Son and Holy Spirit.
May all the angels in the heavens reply:
    Amen! Amen! Amen!
Power, praise, honour, eternal glory
    to God, the only Giver of grace.
    Amen! Amen! Amen!
        Third-century Egyptian doxology[54]

Today, my living, loving, holy God, today my prayer is entirely and explicitly to your praise. Not about my needs and hopes and wants, nor even those of my world. This special day is a day to revel in your praise:

— in the wonder and mystery of your being, Father, Son and Holy Spirit;
— in the wonder and mystery of your relationship with your creation, seen and unseen;
— in the wonder and mystery of your loving design for us.

O holy God, I reflect with awe on the mystery that all things praise you, and that you have created us thus. Small and insignificant as I am, Lord, in the presence of your aweful holiness, yet today I can offer my praise; and my soul can kneel before you.

O loving God, I reflect with joy on the wonder that you love and know the whole vastness of your creation, in its smallest detail. Small and insignificant as I am, Lord, in the presence of that inconceivable love, yet I too can know that love guiding my life: and my soul can kneel before you.

Praise to the holiest in the height,
and in the depth be praise;
In all his words most wonderful,
most sure in all his ways.

                              Amen.
                    J. H. Newman

PRAYER NOTES

Sunday · EVENING

I do not know
what resurrection is
(though I'm almost sure
it has something to do
with hallowing common ground) . . .

I expect one day I'll get up
and find that it sneaked up on me
while I wasn't looking
and maybe even that it's been there all along . . .

In the meantime
I believe in it.

Kathy Galloway[55]

O great and all-holy and most loving God, thank you for today. Thank you for everything in it which has hallowed the common ground of my life. Thank you for your gift of worship, both private and public, and fellow pilgrims to worship among. Thank you for the freedom here to exercise that gift, and forgive me that sometimes I am careless of it. Thank you for words and music that inspire; and for food for my soul in Bible reading and sermon, and in others' shared reflections on their journey with you. Thank you for the light shed today on the profound meaning and potential holiness of our everyday life.

And be with all those tonight, Father, who have spent their energies today in service to your worshipping people: refresh them in your power.

And most dear Father, in the light of this day's sense of renewal, let me grasp afresh that you have made me for eternity and that I live my life in its light. And so, as I think of tomorrow, and prepare myself for sleep tonight, let me know Christ's resurrection power afresh, whether I am sleeping or waking, at Sunday leisure or Monday toil.

And may my life in pilgrimage, through this hallowed ground, be a song of resurrection praise. Amen.

PRAYER NOTES

Seasons and Festivals

Advent

O God that art the only hope of the world,
The only refuge for unhappy men,
Abiding in the faithfulness of heaven,
Give me strong succour in this testing place . . .
Remember I am dust, and wind, and shadow,
And life as fleeting as the flower of grass.
But may the eternal mercy which hath shone
From time of old
Rescue thy servant from the jaws of the lion.
Thou who didst come from on high in the cloak
    of flesh
Strike down the dragon with that two-edged
    sword,
Whereby our mortal flesh can war with winds
And beat down strongholds, with our Captain
    God.

The Venerable Bede[56]

Lord God, as I hear the majestic message of Advent, with its call to prepare for the coming of the Lord Christ, and its reminder of the First and Last Things between which I live; give me grace to use this time well.

Let me recognize and offer my mortality to the transformation of Christ's coming.

Let me recognize and offer my standing under judgement to the transformation of Christ's passion.

Let me recognize and offer the eventual end of all things to the transformation of Christ the King, enthroned in power in realms beyond the world's ending.

So, Lord, let me in sober and thankful wonder prepare myself for your Advent:

Almighty God,
give us grace to cast away the works of darkness

and to put on the armour of light,
now in the time of this mortal life
in which your Son Jesus Christ
    came to us in great humility:
so that on the last day,
when he shall come again in his glorious majesty
    to judge the living and the dead,
we may rise to the life immortal;
through him who is alive and reigns
    with you and the Holy Spirit,
one God, now and forever. Amen.

The Collect for Advent Sunday

Bible Sunday · Advent 2

The Bible

That! That! There I was told
That I the *Son of God* am made,
His Image. O Divine! And that fine gold,
　　With all the joys that here do fade,
Are but a Toy, compared to the Bliss
Which Hev'nly, God-like and Eternal is.
　　That We on earth are Kings;
And, tho' we're cloathed with mortal Skin,
Are Inward Cherubims; hav Angels Wings;
　　Affections, Thoughts and Minds within,
Can soar throu all the Coasts of Hev'n and Earth;
And shall be sated with Celestial Mirth.

Thomas Traherne[57]

O Lord God, thank you for the Bible and its profound influence on the world and on my life.

Lord, I am conscious I live in a society which takes for granted the freedom we have to read and study your word. Yet for so many millions it is not so. Lord, I pray for them that they may not be forever cut off from the lively oracles of God. And for me, that I may be more consciously thankful to you, and grateful to those who fought for this freedom to study the Scriptures.

And Lord God, when I turn to the Bible, help me to recognize its purpose as Thomas Traherne did in this verse. Help me to see it as a guide map to heaven and my heavenly state. Help me to reflect on what it says about my true condition as a loved child of God, and about my heavenly destiny, and about the Lord Christ who made that possible. So let me read it with honesty of mind, not evading its difficulties and contradictions; and with an open heart, looking for the guidance you can give me if I study it in truth and longing.

Give me perseverance, honesty and love in its study, Lord: that I may hear your authentic voice in its pages, and so better understand my creaturely condition as your child. Amen.

Christmas Eve

Moonless darkness stands between.
Past, O Past, no more be seen!
But the Bethlehem star may lead me
To the sight of Him who freed me
From the self that I have been.
Make me pure, Lord: Thou art holy;
Make me meek, Lord: Thou wert lowly;
Now beginning and alway:
Now begin, on Christmas Day.

Gerard Manley Hopkins[58]

Loving Father, now at the climax of this time of waiting I offer to you tonight all my longing and hoping in it. In the silent hours of this night's darkness may the wonder of it all be renewed in me. Let the mystery and holiness of your great gift to us, which tonight we celebrate afresh, come upon me as strangely and gloriously as to the shepherds in the fields near Bethlehem. Tonight, Father.

— let me glimpse the joy of angels at the goodness of God;
— let me know myself freed by this infant Saviour from all I am ashamed of and would leave behind: the guilt of a life selfishly lived, the burden of spoilt relationships, and the misery of failed effort.

Lord God, I bring all these tonight to the poor stable, and ask that in this holy darkness my past may no more be seen, but my present and future be lit by that shining and generous love which shone round the angels as they sang of glory, and which shines for all of us where Christ is born.

Bless tonight, Father, those for whom amidst others' joy this is a hard and bitter time of suffering or remembering, those for whom your gift seems to offer so little comfort. Deepen true care in my heart for them; and for those for whom this night has no holiness or glimpse of the wonder of your love. Thank you that your gift is to us all, and that you patiently await our acceptance. Bring us all, dear Father, at the last to know it and receive it. Amen.

O God, who makest us glad with the yearly remembrance of the birth of Thy only Son, Jesus Christ: Grant that as we joyfully receive Him for our redeemer, so we may with sure confidence behold Him, when He shall come to be our judge: who liveth and reigneth with Thee and the Holy Spirit, one God, world without end. Amen.

Collect for Christmas Eve

Christmas Day

O sweet child of Bethlehem, grant that we may share with all our hearts in this profound mystery of Christmas. Put into the hearts of men this peace for which they sometimes seek so desperately and which you alone can give them. Help them to know one another better, and to live as . . . children of the same Father.

Reveal to them also your beauty, holiness and purity. Awaken in their hearts love and gratitude for your infinite goodness. Join them all together in your love. And give us your heavenly peace.

Pope John XXIII[59]

> O the magnitude of meekness!
>   Worth from worth immortal sprung;
> O the strength of infant weakness,
>   If eternal is so young! . . .
>
> Nature's decorations glisten
>   Far above their usual trim;
> Birds on box and laurel listen,
>   As so near the cherubs hymn . . .
>
> God all-bounteous, all creative,
>   Whom no ills from good dissuade,
> Is incarnate, and a native
>   Of the very world he made.
>   *Christopher Smart*[60]

O God of inconceivable majesty, who chose to make yourself known to us in our own form at its most helpless, dependent and vulnerable, let my Christmas Day prayer be one of wondering thankfulness for the mystery of your gift of yourself. Put into my heart, Father, a spark of your yearning tenderness and compassion and respect for all who are marginalized or

138

hard-pressed or vulnerable. And fan that spark into a flame that burns brightly for my Lord and my fellow-creatures throughout the year. Amen.

Epiphany

Cold on his cradle the dew-drops are shining,
    Low lies his head with the beasts of the stall:
Angels adore him in slumber reclining,
    Maker and monarch and saviour of all.

Say, shall we yield him, in costly devotion,
    Odours of Edom and offerings divine?
Gems of the mountain and pearls of the ocean,
    Myrrh from the forest or gold from the mine?

Vainly we offer each ample oblation,
    Vainly with gifts would his favour secure;
Richer by far is the heart's adoration,
    Dearer to God are the prayers of the poor.
                    Richard Heber[61]

O Lord, I am poor in the gifts of discipleship, and yet I long to bring you gifts which honour you. I thank you that Epiphany is a time of revelation, when you lead us into new understanding, and teach us what offerings you desire.

O Lord God, who guided the Magi by a star, let there be an Epiphany in my heart. Let me make my journey with them, finding you and then returning to my world to live out the consequences.
   Let me carry in my heart an offering to you:

— of myrrh: of all suffering I have experienced undeservedly, and can offer to you in innocence;
— of frankincense: of all worship which goes beyond itself and burns my heart with the fire of pure longing to praise you;
— of gold: all the desire for things, Lord, to be surrendered; all the dreams of security through wealth; all the comfort of prosperity. Lord, 'such gold is cold beside

your fire.'[62] I offer my desire for it, that you may burn it away in my heart.

And like the Magi keep me obedient to your prompting, however perplexed I am by it: so that I accept its guidance for my life. Amen.

Ash Wednesday

Somewhere there is Grace, Lord,
Was I not told it as a child
When the sound of the sparrow
Filled my heart with delight
And the rain fell like friendship on my head.
  Now the call of the cuckoo
Cannot calm my aching heart
And my soul is tormented with fear.
   Have mercy, Lord, for I have travelled far
   Yet all my knowledge is as nothing
   My days are numbered . . .

Forgiveness, O forgive me, Lord,
Close my critical eye
Take me to your breast
For how else may I die?

Cliff Ashby[63]

O almighty Lord, let the solemnity of Ash Wednesday be to me the beginning of a truly heart-searching pilgrimage through Lent. In so much I have lost touch with the real sources of my soul's health and delight. I have let myself drift astray, travelling far but arriving nowhere; and I know I need to see afresh, with the child-like trust that my critical wordliness has blurred, the truths that make for my peace. So forgive me, Lord, all that is past, and all that is ill about what I have become. Draw me to yourself so that I make this Lenten journey guided by you, sure of your astringent mercy and your healing grace. Through Christ my Lord. Amen.

Almighty and everlasting God,
you hate nothing you have made
and forgive the sins of all those who are
  penitent.

142

Create and make in us new and contrite hearts
that, lamenting our sins
   and acknowledging our wretchedness,
we may receive from you, the God of all mercy,
perfect forgiveness and peace;
through Jesus Christ our Lord. Amen.
                              Collect for Ash Wednesday

Lent

Lenten Prayers for Others

God of the heights and the depths
we bring to you
    those driven into the desert,
    those struggling with difficult decisions.
May they choose life.

God of the light and darkness
we bring to you
    those lost in the mist of drugs or drink,
    those dazzled by the use of power
May they choose life.

God of the wild beast and the ministering angel,
we bring to you
    those savaged by others' greed,
    those exhausted by caring for others.
May they feel your healing touch.

Kate McIlhagga[64]

A Lenten prayer for myself

Now quit your care
    And anxious fear and worry;
    For schemes are vain
    And fretting brings no gain.
To prayer, to prayer!
    Bells call and clash and hurry,
        In Lent the bells do cry,
            'Come buy, come buy,
        Come buy with love the love most high!'

Lent comes in the spring,
　　And spring is pied with brightness;
　　　The sweetest flowers,
　　　Keen winds, and sun, and showers,
Their health do bring
　　To make Lent's chastened whiteness;
　　　For life to us brings light
　　　　And might, and might,
　　　And might to those whose hearts are right . . .

To bow the head
　　In sackcloth and in ashes,
　　　Or rend the soul,
　　　Such grief is not Lent's goal;
But to be led
To where God's glory flashes,
　　His beauty to come nigh,
　　　To fly, to fly,
　　To fly where truth and light do lie.

For righteousness
　　And peace will show their faces
　　　To those who feed
　　　The hungry in their need,
And wrongs redress,
　　Who build the old waste places,
　　　And in the darkness shine.
　　　　Divine, divine,
　　　Divine it is when all combine!

Percy Dearmer[65]

Palm Sunday

Jesus, King of the universe;
ride on in humble majesty:

Lord, this Palm Sunday may I recognize in you the Lord
who comes to his world, and join with full heart in the
children's 'hosanna'.

Ride on, through conflict and debate,
ride on through sweaty prayer and betrayal of friends:

Lord, this Palm Sunday forgive me my evasions of truth,
my carelessness of your honour; my weakness which leaves
me sleeping even while in others you suffer and are anguished; my cowardice that does not risk the consequences
of publicly acknowledging you as Lord.

Ride on to the empty tomb and your rising
   in triumph,
Ride on to raise up your Church, a new body
   for your service;
Ride on, King Jesus, to renew the whole
   earth in your image,
in compassion come to help us. Amen.

Based on a prayer used in
Andrha Theological College,
Hyderabad.[66]

Lord, this Palm Sunday may I see in each cross of palm
leaves the new life blossoming from your cross of wood. In
the songs of rejoicing may I hear a faint echo of that greater
and more glorious hymn that lies beyond Easter Day. In the
Palm Sunday procession may I see foreshadowed that vast
multitude which no one can number, giving glory and praise
to you in that life they share with you beyond the empty

tomb. So in this Palm Sunday prepare my heart for the Passion and Easter Sunday, my Lord God. In the name of Jesus who is King. Amen.

Good Friday

Christ, whose bitter agony
was watched from afar by women,
enable us to follow the example
of their persistent love;
that being steadfast in the face of horror,
we may also know the place of resurrection,
in your name. Amen.

Janet Morley[67]

O my Lord Jesus, I cannot bring myself to watch you through this horror: yet their persistent love kept them watching by you to the end. Help me to face the Golgotha truth of human life, Lord; and so discover with wonder that you do not only watch alongside me, but shield me from its full terror with your own body and spirit. So may I join with you and the women in steadfastness: and with them discover that this is a place of redemption.

Lord, let us be with you, wherever you are crucified today,
Wherever the will of man crosses the will of God:
For being God and man, you are stretched out on the cross
of God's purpose and our rebellion.
Where the will to violence crosses God's will for peace,
Where lying and corruption cross God's will for truth,
Where greed and possessiveness cross the use of God's plenty,
Where we live not for others but for ourselves,
Where ugliness and disease cross the will of God for beauty
and well-being,
There let us find you, racked on the cross,
And there let us be with you and share your pain,
And bring about with you, in union with your sacrifice,
That redemption which you are accomplishing in your
passion.

Margaret Cropper[68]

O Lord Jesus, forgive me for the times I have racked you on the cross of God's purpose and my rebellion. Let me gaze at that cross and recognize what my wilfulness has done. So join my grief with your passion, Lord; that with your whole creation I may be redeemed. Amen.

Easter Sunday

O Lord God, our Father, You are the light that can never be put out; and now you give us a light that shall drive away all darkness. You are love without coldness, and you have given us such warmth in our hearts that we can love all whom we meet. You are the life that defies death, and you opened for us the way that leads to eternal life. I am not a great Christian; I am humble and ordinary. But your grace is enough for me. Arouse in me that small degree of joy and thankfulness of which I am capable, that timid faith which I can muster, that cautious obedience which I cannot refuse, and thus bring me to that wholeness of life which you have prepared for all of us through the death and resurrection of your Son.

Do not allow me or any of your children to remain apathetic or indifferent to the wonderful glory of Easter, but let the light of our risen Lord reach every corner of our dull hearts. Of *my* dull heart, Father. Amen.

Karl Barth (adapted)[69]

'Easter St John'

God so loved he gave
God loved so he gave
God loved, he gave so

So teach me to love
So I may love, I'll give
So I may give, I'll love
I may so love to give

Teach me Lord to give,
And loving give, and giving love,

So Thou be gift and love so.

Ascension Day

To complete your seamless robe, and so to complete our
faith, you ascended through the air into the heavens,
before the very eyes of the apostles. In this way you
showed that you are the Lord of all, and are the fulfilment
of all creation. Thus from that moment every human and
every living creature should bow at your name. And, in
the eyes of faith, we can see that all creation proclaims
your greatness.

Bernard of Clairvaux[70]

My Lord Jesus Christ, I do not really begin to understand the
mystery of your Ascension, or how to picture it. Only I know
that there had to be a time when your physical presence must
be withdrawn, for the wider world to encounter your love.
And I know that my tender and suffering Lord, and even my
victoriously risen and observable Lord, must become the aweful and glorious Lord, King beyond time and space, ruling
over all the worlds that are and are to be. And I understand
that at your Ascension you went through the door between
time and eternity.

Only, Lord, I should be full of a sense of loss, if it were not
for being with your disciples as they return to Jerusalem,
not sad, but full of a great joy, bursting into hymns praising God. So Lord, it seems they do not so much see you
leaving them, as taking up your rule over all the unacknow-
ledged bits of their lives, including their wonderings about
eternity. They show such a profound sense of wondering
certainty, Lord, an absoluteness of commitment, devotion
and worship.

So, Lord, like them I return to the city. Fill me too with awe
and praise as you take up your kingly rule: renew within me
the wonder of Ascension Day discipleship. Amen.

Pentecost · Whit Sunday

Holy Spirit,
mighty word of God
inhabit our darkness
brood over our abyss
and speak to our chaos;
that we may breathe with your life
and share your creation
in the power of Jesus Christ. Amen.

Janet Morley[71]

O surging Spirit, mighty wind of God, blow through my heart
today. Let me not fear your energy and force, but welcome it in
my life. Let it disperse all those accretions, those patterns of life
and worship I have come to rely on and take pleasure in for
their own sake rather than as ways to you. Disturb my compla-
cencies, Lord, the things I cling to for security in place of cling-
ing to you. And in their place give me the wonder of your fire,
of God's holy flames above my head and in my heart.

O gentle Spirit, breathing on the face of the waters in those
depths of my heart still unformed and in darkness; in that
deepest part of me where there is still chaos, shape your order
and harmony, bring forth your design in new life.

O creator Spirit, make me a channel of your creative life in
the world. Empower me to help others towards new life: and
enable me to reject all that within me is destructive or malign
or repressive. Let me rejoice selflessly in your creative work in
others, glorying in the wonders of God in other people's lives.
And bond us together in the life and calling of the church,
whose day of birth we celebrate today. Keep us aflame with
your new life for the world. In the love and power of the
triune God, Father, Son and Holy Spirit. Amen.

Times of Sorrow, Times of Joy

Joy and Thanksgiving

Lord, on such a day of thankfulness, I want to offer you my whole heart in song; I want to declare to the whole world how great your kindness has been to me through all my life, and most especially now. O Lord God, how great is my hope in you; how faithful your goodness to me!

All my hope on God is founded;
    he doth still my trust renew.
Me through change and chance he guideth
    only good and only true.
      God unknown
      he alone
calls my heart to be his own.
. . . .

God's great goodness aye endureth,
    deep his wisdom, passing thought:
Splendour, light and life attend him,
    beauty springeth out of naught.
      Evermore
      from his store
new-born worlds rise and adore.

Daily doth th'almighty giver
    bounteous gifts on us bestow;
His desire our soul delighteth
    pleasure leads us where we go.
      Love doth stand
      at his hand;
joy doth wait on his command.

Still from man to God eternal
    sacrifice of praise be done,

High above all praises praising
  for the gift of Christ his Son.
    Christ doth call
    one and all:
ye who follow shall not fall.
  Robert Bridges[72]

'Joy doth wait on your command'; Lord God, you have commanded and given me this great cause for joy. O my dear heavenly Father, may my thanks and joy be windows through which to see the wonders of your ever present grace more clearly, and so to let my life be ruled by it. In this moment of thanksgiving, Lord, may my heart be your own. Amen.

See also pages 10, 18, 26, 30, 54, 78, 80, 124, 136

On a Wedding Day

If ever two were one, then surely we.
If ever man were lov'd by wife, then thee;
If ever wife was happy in a man,
Compare with me ye women if you can.
I prize thy love more than whole mines of gold,
Or all the riches that the East doth hold.
My love is such that rivers cannot quench,
Nor aught but love from thee give recompense.
Thy love is such I can no way repay,
The heavens reward thee manifold, I pray.
Then while we live, in love let's so persever
That, when we live no more, we may live ever.

Ann Bradstreet[73]

Loving God, who made us so mysteriously and marvellously, I thank you this special day for your holy gift of marriage. Father, this is so huge and solemn a change of life: help me to recognize its mystery and yet be so sure of it as your gift and plan that it is full of delight and joy, without shadow and without fear.

O God and Father, thank you for the depths of love in this marriage. May it grow deeper and richer, rooted in your love, so that it transcends at the end this earthly life and points us on to heaven, 'where we may live ever'.

Bless, Lord, the energy and effort that so many people have already put into preparing for today, and give great joy to all those helping or sharing in it. May none of us forget that it is a moment and a rite given and ordained by you; and may all of us sense your presence with us,

— blessing the vows made publicly;
— hallowing the new family coming into being;

156

— comforting the homes left with a gap;
— underwriting with your promise the future here begun.

May your blessing rest on the new home whose life begins today. Sanctify it with your presence, and fill it with peace and love; through Jesus Christ our Lord. Amen.

> Lord, bless us and protect us.
> Lord, smile on us and show us your favour.
> Lord, befriend us and prosper us. Amen.

In Pain

I shall know why, when time is over,
And I have ceased to wonder why;
Christ will explain each separate anguish
In the fair school-room of the sky.

He will tell me what Peter promised,
And I, for wonder at his woe,
I shall forget the drop of anguish
That scalds me now, that scalds me now.

Emily Dickinson[74]

Father God, I have struggled so with this anguish, and I am weary and heart-sick. I do not understand why you permit this suffering, or how it can enrich either the world or me. So now I cry to you as Jesus cried to you: Father, if it may be so, take this terrible burden from me . . .

But Father, taught by him, more than anything I want to hold on to you, and be held by you, even through this. So as I struggle I ask above all that you be with me:

— holding me steady against the tides of anger and despair;
— giving me courage to bear with fortitude;
— strengthening my faith in your ultimate victory over all that has power to hurt us, disease and death, bereavement and loss, penury and betrayal, the unkindness of our fellows, and the vast impersonal forces of societies and nations.

And Father, do not let me be so trapped in my own pain that I cannot look outward to those around me, in compassion or thanksgiving. I pray for others who at this moment groan, or grieve, and ask that the comfort for which I ask may be theirs also.

And I thank you for all those who, by words or deeds of goodness and kindness, have come alongside me and shared my load. Be with them, and let my thanksgiving for them be taken up into your blessing of them. And keep us all safe from that which would destroy the soul. Amen.

See also pages 10, 28, 36, 56, 90

Forgiving

> Forgive us our sins, as we forgive those who
> sin against us.
>
> *The Lord's Prayer*

Father, I cannot do it. I have struggled so long and hard with
my hurt, and my anger and my bitterness, and I can find no
rest. The tempest is swirling in my heart and brain, and I do
not know how to still it. I do not even know that I want to. I
know I want satisfaction. I want justice. I want the whole
matter sorted out so that my rightness is vindicated . . . And
yet a part of me trembles and weeps and longs for reconcilia-
tion and a restored relationship. Lord, I feel so trapped. I
want to escape this coil of unforgiving bitterness; and yet not,
because that would feel like defeat.

Help me to look at you, my Christ, in all this, turning my
eyes away from this tangle of anger and hurt towards you.
You, stretched agonizingly on that Cross, Lord, saying
'Father, forgive'. How did you pray that? Because you
loved and understood us better than we love and understand ourselves? Because you loved our Father God
most of all? Because you knew that the cycle of anger and
resentment can be broken by any of us if in your strength
we long for the other person's good, enough to bear their
injustice to us patiently? O Jesus, give me a heart that
so knows itself forgiven in the love of God and the power
flowing from the Cross, of all that smears and soils
it — and wounds it — that it cannot but be itself for-
giving. Make me aware of the great surging sea of forgiveness in which I, with this whole world, am borne along
by your marvellous grace; and so carried and cradled,
prompt in me an offering to you of that same forgiveness to
others. So that I can with truth and yearning kneel before
you — now — and with all my heart pray, 'Father, as I

forgive those who have offended me, so, forgive me for my offences also.' Amen.

See also pages 43, 66, 92, 110

On My Birthday

A birthday thanksgiving and commitment:

> When all thy mercies, O my God
> my rising soul surveys
> transported with the view I'm lost
> in wonder, love and praise.

Lord, I look back on my birthdays through the past, and marvel at the way of grace of which they are the milestones. Thank you, Lord.

> Unnumbered comforts to my soul
> thy tender care bestowed,
> before my infant heart conceived
> from whom those comforts flowed.

Lord, in my childhood I knew love and was kept secure. Then I did not know you and could not praise you. Now I know you, praise you and thank you. And ask for your tenderest mercy on all those little ones who are neglected, unloved, abused or sick. Guide to them, Lord, those who bring help and healing.

> When in the slippery paths of youth
> with heedless steps I ran,
> thine arm unseen conveyed me safe,
> and led me up to man
> . . . .

Lord, I did not understand in those years the dangers among which I moved, or how slippery were the paths of youthful idealism and hope. Thank you for guarding me, Lord, and for picking me up whenever I fell. And guard those who follow me into that confusing world of intense hope and joy, and vulnerable sensitivity to pain, rejection and despair.

Through every period of my life
thy goodness I'll pursue,
and after death in distant worlds
the glorious theme renew.

Through all eternity to thee
a joyful song I'll raise;
for O, eternity's too short
to utter all thy praise.

Lord, I do not know how many more birthdays lie before me.
I only know that you will be with me in each of them, your
goodness supplying me. And that beyond them lies all eternity, to tell out my joy. So let my birthdays be always associ-
ated in my heart with praise to you, my Lord. Amen.

Based on hymn by Joseph Addison[75]

In Despair

Do not lose your servant who you have
sought and found in the abyss of hell
    where no one is found.
I hear Lord that you order me to come forth
    but I cannot get out,
miserably bound and weighted down with so
    great a weight.

Anselm of Canterbury[76]

'He descended into hell . . . .'

Lord, I am deadened: there is no hope or light or joy in the
world. I know others feel hope, but their words to me are
meaningless. I know I once had hope and light and joy myself,
but they are all gone. All I know is this heavy hard lump in my
heart, this sense of blackness everywhere. Even things that
gave me joy, like the love of my family, or my friends, or my
pets; or music or books or radio and TV; or walking on the
green hillsides or by the river: even these do not move the
darkness. Worst of all, I can't move towards *you*, Lord. I hear
your voice in all these things I loved, ordering me to 'come
forth': but I cannot get out.

    I cannot get out. I cannot get out.

. . . As though I am bound tight in a great chain that weighs
me down and fastens me in.

    Lord of Lazarus:
    Lord of the empty tomb:

. . . I cannot get out, so you must come in.

        you must come in

come and break down this door, so that I see some light; come in and loosen my chain so the weight slips off me, and I can put my hand in yours and walk out.

O Lord, I am in an abyss of hell: *but you have been there too*.
Come in, come in, Lord, to this place you once redeemed.
And save me.   Amen.

Loss and Bereavement

O God, who brought us to birth,
and in whose arms we die,
in our grief and shock
contain and comfort us;
embrace us with your love,
give us hope in our confusion,
and grace to let go into new life,
through Jesus Christ, Amen.
Janet Morley[77]

They are all gone into the world of light!
   And I alone sit ling'ring here;
Their very memory is fair and bright,
   And my sad thoughts doth clear

. . . .

I see them walking in an air of glory,
   Whose light doth trample on my days:
My days, which are at best but dull and hoary,
   Mere glimmering and decays

. . . .

Dear beauteous death! the jewel of the just,
   Shining nowhere but in the dark;
What mysteries do lie beyond thy dust;
   Could man outlook that mark!

. . . .

O Father of eternal life, and all
   Created glories under thee!
Resume thy spirit from this world of thrall
   Into true liberty.

Either disperse these mists, which blot and fill
   My perspective (still) as they pass,
Or else remove me hence unto that hill
   Where I shall need no glass.

Henry Vaughan[78]

O Lord God, this loss hurts so. My dead are so alive, I cannot believe I cannot touch them or speak to them. I so want them, Father, so miss them . . . I *bleed*, Father. Help me; help me in this fog, which blots out my perspective on the life they now live in your hereafter. Give me hope, dear Lord God, give me hope in Christ's own defeat of death, that one day I shall see my loved ones again; and touch them and hear them, not in the vividness of my mind's eye; not in dreams or memories; but in that world of light to which, O my loving Lord, safely bring me. Amen.

In Old Age

The prayer of the old horse

See, Lord,
my coat hangs in tatters,
like homespun, old, threadbare.
All that I had of zest,
all my strength,
I have given in hard work
and kept nothing back for myself.
Now
my poor head swings
to offer up all the loneliness of my heart.
Dear God,
stiff on my thickened legs
I stand here before You:
Your unprofitable servant.*
Oh! of your goodness
give me a gentle death. Amen.
Carmen Bernes de Gasztold[79]

'Je suis Votre serviteur inutile!'* . . . O my Lord God, that is
the awful burden I feel in ageing: that I am your useless servant. My body is lumpish and clumsy, its beauty gone: I am
stiff on my thickened legs, and cannot speed about serving
others and you. My thoughts seem not to come out clearly,
and I irritate others by my slowness in speech and decision
and action. And Lord so many of my family and friends aren't
here any more — I look about me and it's lonely, Lord. The
past was full of laughter and companionship and hope and
energy and service. Now my world has contracted to this
small space. O Lord, I'm little use to you, and a burden to
others.

So help me, Lord. Help me to bear it graciously. Help me to
remember the past not with nostalgia but with thankfulness.

Help me:

— to suffer diminishments of body and mind and activity with humour and detachment;
— to offer the gifts of old age: time, leisure, quiet, tolerance, understanding and love, to your glory and the service of others, by using them in the way I still can, in praying and in caring;
— to accept dependency graciously when it must come, letting it remind me that I have always been utterly dependent on you;
— never to criticise when I can praise;
— never to complain when I can thank;
— never to despair when I can hope;
— and to offer these to you and others for Christ's sake. Amen.

Approaching Death

On first knowing that death is likely:

O God, comfort and help me.
Give me strength to bear what you send,
And do not let fear rule over me.
As a loving Father take care of my loved ones . . .

O merciful God,
Forgive all the sins I have committed
Against you and my fellows.
I put my trust in your grace,
And commit my life wholly into your hands.
Do with me as is best for you,
For that will be best for me too.
Whether I live or die, I am with you,
And you are with me.
Lord, I wait for your salvation
And for your kingdom.

Dietrich Bonhoeffer,
(on being condemned to death)[80]

When death is very near

Lord, I know I am near the end:
Stay with me, my Lord.
I know that dying is my last big task for you:
Stay with me, my Lord.
As you have helped me in my living,
So keep me faithful in my dying:
Stay with me, my Lord.
However its dread or pain may seize me,
Lassitude, chill, darkness overwhelm me,
Even as disintegrating appals me,

Lord,
Even then,
Stay with me, my Lord.
Help me, O help me, to make
An offering of it to you,
O Lord of my death as well as my life.
O Christ my Lord, O Jesus my Lord,
Give me a holy death.

A commendation to God's care in whatever lies beyond.

Bring me, O Lord God, at my last awakening, into the house
and gate of heaven, to enter into that gate and dwell in that
house, where there shall be no darkness nor dazzling but one
equal light; no noise nor silence but one equal music; no fears
nor hopes but one equal posession; no ends nor beginnings
but one equal eternity; in the habitations of thy glory and
dominion world without end. Amen.

John Donne (adapted)[81]

See also pp36, 120/21, 132

Envoi

Go forth upon thy journey, Christian soul!
Go from this world! Go, in the name of God
The omnipotent Father who created thee!
Go, in the name of Jesus Christ, our Lord,
Son of the living God, who bled for thee!
Go, in the name of the Holy Spirit, who
Hath been poured out on thee! Go, in the name
Of Angels and Archangels; in the name
Of Thrones and Dominations; in the name
Of Princedoms and of Powers; and in the name
Of Cherubim and Seraphim, go forth!
Go, in the name of Patriarchs and Prophets;
And of Apostles and Evangelists,
Of Martyrs and Confessors; in the name
Of holy Monks and Hermits; in the name
Of holy Virgins; and all Saints of God,
Both men and women, go! Go on thy course!
And may thy place today be found in peace,
And may thy dwelling be the Holy Mount
Of Sion: through the same, through Christ, our Lord.

J. H. Newman[82]

PRAYER NOTES

PRAYER NOTES

REFERENCES

All material not otherwise attributed, whether verse or prose, is by Ruth Etchells.

1. Guigo the Carthusian (d.1188), *The Ladder of Monks*, trans. E. Colledge and J. Walsh.
2. Boethius (480–524), trans. Helen Waddell, *More Latin Lyrics*, ed. Dame Felicitas Corrigan (Gollancz 1976).
3. Adapted from Lancelot Andrewes (1555–1626), from *Bishop Andrewe's Devotions*, ed. Edmund Venables (Suttaby & Co. 1883).
4. Thomas Merton, (1915–1968).
5. St Patrick, version in *Songs of Praise* (OUP, 1959 impression).
6. The Venerable Bede (672–735), displayed over his tomb in Durham Cathedral.
7. David Adam (1936–), *Tides and Seasons*, (Triangle 1989).
8. Dag Hammarskjold (1905–61), trans. Leif Sjoberg, and W. H. Auden, *Markings* (Faber and Faber 1964).
9. Michel Quoist (1921–), *Prayers of Life*, (Gill and Macmillan Ltd 1965).
10. William Cowper (1731–1800), 'God moves in a mysterious way', *Olney Hymns*, 1779. Reprinted in *William Cowper, Selected Poems*, ed. Nick Rhodes (Carcanet Press 1984).
11. R. S. Thomas (1913–), 'Reply', in *Experimenting with an Amen* (Macmillan 1993).
12. From *The Lion Book of Famous Prayers*, (Lion 1983).
13. Abp. Helder Camara (1909–), 'King's Son', *Into Your Hands, Lord* (Darton, Longman & Todd 1987).
14. Julian of Norwich (*c*.1332–*c*.1420), *Revelations of Divine Love*, trans. C. Wolters (Penguin 1973).
15. W. H. Auden (1907–74), 'Anthem' (1972), in *W H Auden, Collected Poems*, ed. Edward Mendelson (Faber and Faber 1976).
16. Amy Carmichael (1867–1951), *Gold Cord*, (SPCK 1932).
17. Kathy Galloway, 'Doing Love' in *Love Burning Deep* (SPCK 1993).
18. Walter de la Mare (1873–1956), 'Shadow', in *Complete Poems* (Faber and Faber 1969). Copyright: The Literary Trustees of Walter de la Mare, and The Society of Authors as their representative.

19. Jacob Boehme (1575–1624), *The Way to Christ* trans. P. C. Erb.
20. Anselm of Canterbury (*c.*1033–1109), in *The Prayers and Meditations of Saint Anselm*, trans. Benedicta Ward (Penguin 1973).
21. Julian of Norwich, see Note 14.
22. Thomas Ken (1637–1711), in *Hymns Ancient and Modern, New Standard*, (Hymns Ancient and Modern 1983).
23. Carmen Bernos de Gasztold, trans. Rumer Godden, in *Prayers from the Ark* (Macmillan 1962, Pan Books, revised 1992).
24. Freely adapted from John Baillie (1886–1960), *A Diary of Private Prayer* (OUP 1936).
25. Corrie ten Boom, (1892–1983), in *Women of Prayer*, ed. Dorothy M. Stewart (Collins Fount 1993).
26. Anselm of Canterbury, see Note 20.
27. Freely adapted from Leslie Weatherhead (1883–1975), *A Private House of Prayer* (Arthur James 1985).
28. Frank Topping (1937–   ), *Lord of Life* (The Lutterworth Press 1982). By permission of Curtis Brown Ltd, London.
29. Esther de Waal, *Seeking God* (Collins Fount 1984).
30. Charles Wesley (1707–88), 'O Thou who camest from above', in *Hymns Ancient and Modern, New Standard*, see Note 22.
31. John Donne (1572–1631), from *Divine Poems* ed. Helen Gardner (OUP 1979).
32. Margaret Cropper (1886–1980), *New Life: A Book of Prayers* (Longman 1942).
33. R. S. Thomas, 'Gift', in *Experimenting with an Amen*, see Note 11.
34. John Keble (1792–1866), from 'Morning Hymn', reprinted in *The New Oxford Book of Christian Verse*, ed. Donald Davie (OUP 1981).
35. *The Iona Community Worship Book*, Graham Maule and John Bell, (Wild Goose Publications, Glasgow 1991).
36. Frank Topping, see Note 28.
37. Thomas Fuller (1608–61), reprinted in *Uncommon Prayers*, ed. Cecil Hunt (Hodder and Stoughton 1963).
38. Anonymous prayer from the concentration camp at Ravensbruck, *c.*1944.
39. John Baillie, see Note 24.
40. Michel Quoist, see Note 9.
41. Julian of Norwich, see Note 14.

42. Adapted from George Appleton (1902–1993) in *The Word Is Seed* (SPCK 1976).

43. Cliff Ashby, 'Latter Day Psalms', in *Plain Song: Collected Poems* (Carcanet Press Ltd 1985).

44. From *Celtic Fire*, (prayers *c*.450–*c*.700), ed. R. Van de Weyer (Darton, Longman and Todd 1990).

45. Kathy Galloway, 'Monday: up against the wall', in *Love Burning Deep*, see Note 17.

46. Based on a prayer by Bishop Jacob of Travancore, South India, in *Morning, Noon and Night*, ed. John Carden (CMS 1976).

47. Sir Thomas More (1478–1535), reprinted in *The Oxford Book of Prayer*, ed. G. Appleton (OUP 1985).

48. William Langland (?1330–1400), *The Book Concerning Piers the Plowman*, trans. Donald Attwater, in *The New Oxford Book of Christian Verse*, see Note 34.

49. William Baldwin (*fl.* 1547–49), *The Canticles or Ballads of Solomon*, 1549, in *The New Oxford Book of Christian Verse*, see Note 34.

50. Abd Ab' Azuz Al-Dirini, from 'Purity of Heart', in *Morning, Noon, and Night*, see Note 46.

51. J. H. Newman (1801–90), *Oxford Book of Prayer*, see Note 47.

52. Source unknown; collected in *Morning, Noon, and Night*, see Note 46.

53. Olivia Michael, collected in *New Christian Poetry*, ed. Alwyn Marriage (Collins Flame 1990).

54. Anon, (3rd–6th centuries), in *Early Christian Prayers*, ed. A. Hamman (Longman 1961).

55. Kathy Galloway, 'Sunday: Resurrection', in *Love Burning Deep*, see Note 17.

56. Adapted from the Venerable Bede (672–735), trans. Helen Waddell, in *More Latin Lyrics*, see Note 2.

57. Thomas Traherne (1637–74), in *The Penguin Book of English Christian Verse*, ed. Peter Levi (Penguin 1984).

58. Gerard Manley Hopkins (1844–89), *Poems of Gerard Manley Hopkins*, ed. Bridges and Gardner (OUP 1918, 3rd imp. of 3rd edn, 1950).

59. Pope John XXIII (1881–1963), *Journal of a Soul*, trans. Dorothy White (Geoffrey Chapman 1980).

60. Christopher Smart (1722–71), from Hymn 32 in *Hymns and Spiritual Songs for the Feasts and Festivals of the Church of England*, in *The New Oxford book of Christian Verse*, see Note 34.
61. Richard Heber (1783–1826), from 'Brightest and best of the sons of the morning', in *Songs of Praise* (OUP 1936).
62. Alwyn Marriage, from 'Epiphany' in *Beautiful Man* (Outpost Publications 1977).
63. Cliff Ashby, from 'Latter Day Psalms', see Note 43 above.
64. Kate McIlhagga, from *Encompassing Presence* the Prayer Handbook for 1993 (United Reformed Church 1993).
65. Percy Dearmer, from 'White Lent' in *Songs of Praise*, see Note 61. In line 16 'us' replaces 'man'.
66. Based on prayer used by Andrha Theological College, Hyderabad, in 'Services for all Seasons', reprinted in *Morning Noon and Night*, see Note 46.
67. Janet Morley, from *All Desires Known* (SPCK 1988).
68. Margaret Cropper (1886–1980), from *Draw Near* (SPCK 1935).
69. Karl Barth (1886–1968), *Call of God*, trans. A. T. Mackay, (SCM Press).
70. Bernard of Clairvaux (1090–1153), *On the Christian Year*, trans. by a Religious from CSMV.
71. Janet Morley, see Note 67.
72. Robert Bridges (1844–1930), based on German of J. Neander (1650–80), reprinted in *Hymns Ancient and Modern, New Standard*, see Note 22.
73. Ann Bradstreet (1612–72), reprinted in *Faith in her Words*, ed. Veronica Zundel (Lion 1991).
74. Emily Dickinson (1830–36), *The Poems of Emily Dickinson*, ed. Thomas H. Johnson (The Belknap Press of Harvard University 1955).
75. Based on Joseph Addison (1672–1719), in *Hymns Ancient and Modern, New Standard*, see Note 22.
76. Anselm of Canterbury, see Note 20.
77. Janet Morley, see Note 67.
78. Henry Vaughan (1621–95), 'The Ascencion Hymn', in *The Metaphysical Poets of the Seventeenth Century*, ed. H. J. C. Grierson (Clarendon Press 1924).
79. Carmen Bernos de Gasztold, *Prayers from the Ark*, see Note 23.

80. Dietrich Bonhoeffer, (1906–45) *Fiction from Prison*, trans. C. Green (Fortress 1981).
81. John Donne, (1572–31), in *The Oxford Book of Prayer*, see note 47.
82. John Henry Newman, (1801–90) from 'The Dreams of Gerontius', in *Verses on Various Occasions* (Burns and Oates 1867).

THEMATIC INDEX

AUTHOR INDEX

The PRAYING WITH series
A series of books making accessible the words of some
of the great characters and traditions of faith for
use by all Christians.
There are 14 titles in the series, including:

PRAYING WITH SAINT AUGUSTINE
Introduction by Murray Watts

PRAYING WITH SAINT FRANCIS
Introduction by David Ford

PRAYING WITH THE NEW TESTAMENT
Introduction by Joyce Huggett

PRAYING WITH SAINT TERESA
Introduction by Elaine Storkey

PRAYING WITH THE OLD TESTAMENT
Introduction by Richard Holloway

PRAYING WITH THE ENGLISH MYSTICS
Compiled and Introduced by Jenny Robertson

PRAYING WITH THE ENGLISH POETS
Compiled and Introduced by Ruth Etchells

PRAYING WITH THE MARTYRS
Preface by Madeleine L'Engle

PRAYING WITH JOHN DONNE AND
GEORGE HERBERT
Preface by Richard Harries

Books by Frank Colquhoun

PRAYERS FOR TODAY

A modern book of prayers dealing with matters of common
experience. Divided into three sections, the prayers cover
personal life, the Christian pilgrimage and a broad range of
public issues. Many of the prayers are also suitable for use in
church or group worship.

PRAYERS FOR EVERYONE

A wide-ranging collection offering prayers for many
different situations. Prayers of Christian faith and devotion
are gathered together with some for everyday needs and
others showing a concern for the world around us. The book
also includes a special section of Celtic material.

FAMILY PRAYERS

Prayers and thanksgivings for all family occasions – from
times of joy or of sadness; of celebration or of change; from
the birth of a new baby to the loss of a grandparent. There
are also prayers for friends, neighbours, the local community
and the church fellowship.

Other Triangle books:

PRAYERS FOR PILGRIMS
Compiled by Margaret Pawley
Foreword by David Adam

A unique collection of prayers from different places of
pilgrimage in Britain and all over the world, as well as
prayers about the Christian life as a pilgrim journey.

SEASONS OF THE SPIRIT
Readings through the Christian year
Selected and edited by George Every, Richard Harries,
Kallistos Ware

A rich and varied selection of meditations, poems and
prayers from the Anglican, Roman Catholic and Orthodox
Christian traditions.

TO BE A PILGRIM
A Spiritual Notebook
by Basil Hume

A unique series of spiritual readings by the Cardinal
Archbishop of Westminster.

OUT OF THE ORDINARY
Calligraphy and Meditations

A delightful series of meditations on everyday objects. From
a cup to a flower to a table, Anthea Dove enables her readers
to find God's blessings in the ordinary stuff of life.
Includes calligraphy by Christina Caldwell

TRiANGLE
Books
can be obtained from
all good bookshops.
In case of difficulty,
or for a complete list of our books,
contact:
SPCK Mail Order
36 Steep Hill
Lincoln
LN2 1LU
(tel: 0522 527 486)